Asia Struggles with Democracy

Since 1974, when the current wave of democratization began, the movement toward democracy in Asia has remained limited. Many countries in Asia have not made a decisive move toward democracy and find themselves struggling with the challenges of democratic consolidation and governance. Focusing on Indonesia, Thailand and Korea, this book analyzes why democratization seems to be so difficult in Asia.

The book investigates the dynamics by which citizens embrace democratic rule and reject authoritarianism, and compares these dynamics with those of consolidating democracies around the world. It also inquires about the forces that affect the emergence and stability of democracy, such as elite interactions, economic development and popular attitudes as beliefs and perceptions about the legitimacy of political systems have long been recognized as some of the most critical influences on regime change. Finally, this book discusses what it is about the nature of public opinion and the processes of day-to-day democratic participation that make countries vulnerable to crises of legitimacy. Using Indonesia, Korea and Thailand as case studies, the volume highlights the uniqueness of Asia's path to democracy and outlines both the challenges and opportunities in getting there.

The book will be of interest to students and scholars of Asian politics, comparative politics and international studies.

Giovanna Maria Dora Dore is a Visiting Scholar in the SAIS-JHU Southeast Asia Studies Program. Earlier in her career, she worked for the World Bank Group as a political economist focusing on Asian emerging markets and as Special Assistant to the President.

Routledge Contemporary Asia Series

1 **Taiwan and Post-Communist Europe**
Shopping for allies
Czeslaw Tubilewicz

2 **The Asia-Europe Meeting**
The theory and practice of interregionalism
Alfredo C. Robles, Jr

3 **Islamic Legitimacy in a Plural Asia**
Edited by Anthony Reid and Michael Gilsenan

4 **Asian-European Relations**
Building blocks for global governance?
Edited by Jürgen Rüland, Gunter Schubert, Günter Schucher and Cornelia Storz

5 *Taiwan's Environmental Struggle*
Toward a green Silicon Island
Jack F. Williams and Ch'ang-yi David Chang

6 **Taiwan's Relations with Mainland China**
A tail wagging two dogs
Su Chi

7 **The Politics of Civic Space in Asia**
Building urban communities
Edited by Amrita Daniere and Mike Douglass

8 **Trade and Contemporary Society Along the Silk Road**
An ethno-history of Ladakh
Jacqueline Fewkes

9 **Lessons from the Asian Financial Crisis**
Edited by Richard Carney

10 **Kim Jong Il's Leadership of North Korea**
Jae-Cheon Lim

11 **Education as a Political Tool in Asia**
Edited by Marie Lall and Edward Vickers

12 **Human Genetic Biobanks in Asia**
Politics of trust and scientific advancement
Edited by Margaret Sleeboom-Faulkner

13 **East Asian Regionalism from a Legal Perspective**
Current features and a vision for the future
Edited by Tamio Nakamura

14 **Dissent and Cultural Resistance in Asia's Cities**
Edited by Melissa Butcher and Selvaraj Velayutham

15 **Preventing Corruption in Asia**
Institutional design and policy capacity
Edited by Ting Gong and Stephen Ma

16 **Expansion of Trade and FDI in Asia**
Strategic and policy challenges
Edited by Julien Chaisse and Philippe Gugler

17 **Business Innovation in Asia**
Knowledge and technology networks from Japan
Dennis McNamara

18 **Regional Minorities and Development in Asia**
Edited by Huhua Cao and Elizabeth Morrell

19 **Regionalism in China-Vietnam Relations**
Institution-building in the Greater Mekong subregion
Oliver Hensengerth

20 **From Orientalism to Postcolonialism**
Asia-Europe and the lineages of difference
Edited by Sucheta Mazumdar, Kaiwar Vasant and Thierry Labica

21 **Politics and Change in Singapore and Hong Kong**
Containing contention
Stephan Ortmann

22 **Inter-Ethnic Dynamics in Asia**
Considering the Other through ethnonyms, territories and rituals
Edited by Christian Culas and François Robinne

23 **Asia and Latin America**
Political, economic and multilateral relations
Edited by Jörn Dosch and Olaf Jacob

24 **Japan and Africa**
Globalization and foreign aid in the 21st Century
Edited by Howard P. Lehman

25 **De-Westernizing Communication Research**
Altering questions and changing frameworks
Edited by Georgette Wang

26 **Asian Cities, Migrant Labor and Contested Spaces**
Edited by Tai-Chee Wong and Jonathan Rigg

27 **Diaspora Literature and Visual Culture**
Asia in flight
Sheng-mei Ma

28 **Alterities in Asia**
Reflections on identity and regionalism
Edited by Leong Yew

29 **Soft Power in Japan-China Relations**
State, sub-state and non-state relations
Utpal Vyas

30 **Enhancing Asia-Europe Co-operation through Educational Exchange**
Georg Wiessala

31 **History Textbooks and the Wars in Asia**
Divided memories
Edited by Gi-Wook Shin and Daniel C. Sneider

32 **The Politics of Religion in South and Southeast Asia**
Edited by Ishtiaq Ahmed

33 **The Chinese/Vietnamese Diaspora**
Revisiting the boatpeople
Edited by Yuk Wah Chan

34 **The Dynamics of Social Capital and Civic Engagement in Asia**
Vibrant societies
Edited by Amrita Daniere and Hy Van Luong

35 **Eurasia's Ascent in Energy and Geopolitics**
Rivalry or partnership for China, Russia and Central Asia?
Edited by Robert E. Bedeski and Niklas Swanström

36 **Asian Popular Culture in Transition**
Edited by John A. Lent and Lorna Fitzsimmons

37 **Sexual Diversity in Asia, c. 600–1950**
Edited by Raquel Reyes and William G. Clarence Smith

38 **Asia's Role in Governing Global Health**
Edited by Kelley Lee, Tikki Pang and Yeling Tan

39 **Asian Heritage Management**
Contexts, concerns, and prospects
Edited by Kapila D. Silva and Neel Kamal Chapagain

40 **Genocide and Mass Atrocities in Asia**
Legacies and prevention
Edited by Deborah Mayerson and Annie Pohlman

41 **Child Security in Asia**
The impact of armed conflict in Cambodia and Myanmar
Cecilia Jacob

42 **Vietnamese-Chinese Relationships at the Borderlands**
Trade, tourism and cultural politics
Yuk Wah Chan

43 **Asianism and the Politics of Regional Consciousness in Singapore**
Leong Yew

44 **Disaster Relief in the Asia Pacific**
Agency and resilience
Edited by Minako Sakai, Edwin Jurriëns, Jian Zhang and Alec Thornton

45 **Human Trafficking in Asia**
Forcing Issues
Edited by Sallie Yea

46 **Democracy or Alternative Political Systems in Asia**
After the Strongmen
Edited by Michael Hsin-Huang Hsiao

47 **European Studies in Asia**
Contours of a discipline
Georg Wiessala

48 **Corporate Social Responsibility and Human Rights in Asia**
Robert J. Hanlon

49 **Irregular Migration and Human Security in East Asia**
Edited by Jiyoung Song and Alistair D. B. Cook

50 **Renewable Energy in East Asia**
Towards a new developmentalism
Christopher M. Dent

51 **East Asian Development Model**
21st century perspectives
Edited by Shiping Hua and Ruihua Hu

52 **Land Grabs in Asia**
What Role for the Law?
Edited by Connie Carter and Andrew Harding

53 **Asia Struggles with Democracy**
Evidence from Indonesia, Korea and Thailand
Giovanna Maria Dora Dore

54 **China-Malaysia Relations and Foreign Policy**
Razak Abdullah

Asia Struggles with Democracy
Evidence from Indonesia, Korea and Thailand

Giovanna Maria Dora Dore

LONDON AND NEW YORK

First published 2016 by Routledge

2 Park Square, Milton Park, Abingdon, Oxfordshire OX14 4RN
711 Third Avenue, New York, NY 10017

Routledge is an imprint of the Taylor & Francis Group, an informa business

First issued in paperback 2018

Copyright © 2016 Giovanna Maria Dora Dore

The right of Giovanna Maria Dora Dore to be identified as author of this work has been asserted by her in accordance with sections 77 and 78 of the Copyright, Designs and Patents Act 1988.

All rights reserved. No part of this book may be reprinted or reproduced or utilised in any form or by any electronic, mechanical, or other means, now known or hereafter invented, including photocopying and recording, or in any information storage or retrieval system, without permission in writing from the publishers.

Notice:
Product or corporate names may be trademarks or registered trademarks, and are used only for identification and explanation without intent to infringe.

British Library Cataloguing in Publication Data
A catalogue record for this book is available from the British Library

Library of Congress Cataloging-in-Publication Data
Dore, Giovanna Maria Dora.
 Asia struggles with democracy : evidence from Indonesia, Korea and Thailand / Giovanna Maria Dora Dore.
  pages cm
 1. Democracy—Asia. 2. Democracy—Asia—Case studies. 3. Democracy—Indonesia. 4. Democracy—Korea. 5. Democracy—Thailand. I. Title.
 JQ36.D67 2016
 320.95—dc23
 2015005222

ISBN: 978-1-138-83352-4 (hbk)
ISBN: 978-1-138-31967-7 (pbk)

Typeset in Times New Roman
by Apex CoVantage, LLC

Contents

List of illustrations		viii
List of annex illustrations		ix
About the author		xi
1	Introduction	1
2	What does democracy mean to you?	9
3	Is democracy a process or an outcome?	39
4	Does democracy spread like a wave in Asia?	53
5	Is democracy the only game in town?	68
6	Conclusions	97
	Annex 1: the 2000 and 2011 SAIS Surveys	103
	Annex 2: statistical and spatial econometric analyses	109
	Bibliography	141
	Index	155

Illustrations

Figures

5.1	Democratic and authoritarian attitudes in Indonesia, Korea and Thailand	78
5.2	National and capital-level democratic and authoritarian affective support in Indonesia, Korea and Thailand (2011)	80
5.3	Democratic and authoritarian affective support in Seoul, Bangkok and Jakarta in 2000 and 2011	81

Tables

2.1	CSOs membership and participation in Thailand in 2011	35
3.1	Citizens' understanding of democracy in Indonesia, Korea and Thailand	42
3.2	Vote turnout rates for parliamentary elections in Thailand (1946–2007)	49
4.1	Citizens' knowledge of Asian authoritarian regimes in Indonesia, Korea and Thailand	58
4.2	Citizens' knowledge of Asian democratic regimes in Indonesia, Korea and Thailand	60
4.3	Knowledge index for Asian authoritarian and democratic political systems	62
5.1	Preferences for democracy and authoritarianism in Indonesia, Korea and Thailand	74
5.2	World Value Survey preferences for democracy and authoritarianism in Indonesia, Korea and Thailand	76
5.3	Factors influencing citizens' affective support for authoritarianism and democracy	84

Annex illustrations

2.1 Indonesia 2011 summary results for correlations and significance of associations for respondents' democratic cognitive skills — 111

2.2 Indonesia 2011 summary results for logistic regression model for respondents' democratic cognitive skills — 112

2.3 Korea 2011 summary results for correlations and significance of associations for democratic cognitive skills — 113

2.4 Korea 2011 logistic regression model for predictors of citizens' democratic cognitive skills — 114

2.5 Thailand 2011 summary results for correlations and association of significance for democratic cognitive skills — 115

2.6 Thailand 2011 summary results for the logistic regression model for respondents' democratic cognitive skills — 116

2.7 Indonesia 2011 summary results for correlations and significance of associations for democracy as a process or as an outcome — 117

2.8 Indonesia 2011 summary results for the logistic regression model for democracy as a process or an outcome — 118

2.9 Korea 2011 summary results for correlations and significance of associations for democracy as a process or as an outcome — 119

2.10 Korea 2011 summary results for logistic regression model for democracy as a process or an outcome — 120

2.11 Thailand 2011 summary results for correlations and significance of associations for democracy as a process or as an outcome — 121

2.12 Thailand 2011 summary results for logistic regression model for democracy as a process or as an outcome — 122

x *Annex illustrations*

2.13	Indonesia 2011 democracy scale raw scores	123
2.14	Indonesia 2011 democratic scale	124
2.15	Indonesia 2011 summary results for correlations and significance of association for the ID 2011 democracy scale	125
2.16	Summary results for logistic regression model for Indonesia 2011 democracy scale	126
2.17	Korea 2011 democracy scale raw scores	127
2.18	Marginal distribution for Korea 2011 scale of democratic and authoritarian attitudes	128
2.19	Summary results for correlations and significance of association for the Korea 2011 democracy scale	129
2.20	Summary results for logistic regression model for Korea 2011 democracy scale	130
2.21	Thailand 2011 democracy scale raw scores	131
2.22	Thailand 2011 democracy scale	132
2.23	Summary results for correlations and significance of associations for Thailand 2011 democracy scale	133
2.24	Summary results logistic regression model for Thailand 2011 democracy scale	134
2.25	List of countries used in the SAR and SEM analyses	137

About the author

Giovanna Maria Dora Dore is a Visiting Scholar in the Southeast Asia Studies Program at the Paul H. Nitze School of Advanced International Studies of the Johns Hopkins University. Earlier in her career, she has worked as a political economist for the World Bank Group, where she focused on economic and institutional development in the Asia region and also served as Special Assistant to the President. Dr. Dore has lectured at the London School of Economics and Political Science and Johns Hopkins-SAIS on international development, democratization and comparative Asian politics. Giovanna holds a Ph.D. in Political Economy and Southeast Asia Studies (2012) and a M.A. in International Economics and International Relations (1998) from the Paul H. Nitze School of Advanced International Studies of the Johns Hopkins University, a B.A.-M.A. in Philosophy and Contemporary History (1995) from the Catholic University of Milan and an International Baccalaureate Diploma from the United World College of the Adriatic.

1 Introduction

Many countries in Asia are not making a decisive move toward democracy. They remain in a "democratization gray area", with weak political institutions and limited citizens' political engagement. Recently democratized countries in the region find themselves struggling with the challenges of democratic consolidation and governance, whereas authoritarian regimes seem to cope easily with any new challenges emerging from a more globalized regional outlook.

Since 1974, when the current wave of democratization begun, the movement toward democracy in Asia has remained limited, with 8 countries becoming electoral democracies out of more than 60 countries that became democratic around the world.[1] Why does democratization seem so difficult in Asia? For many years, Korea vacillated between parliamentary and military governments until it completed its transition to democracy with the 1987 direct presidential elections. In 1986, People Power ended President Marcos' era and brought the Philippines back to electoral democracy after 14 years of martial law. Yet, since then, the Filipino democracy continued to encounter significant obstacles to consolidation caused by both a weak institutional structure and imperfect constitutional governance. In 1991, Mongolia transitioned to democracy following the collapse of the former Soviet Union. While there is agreement that Mongolia has done well out of necessity of becoming a democracy almost overnight, the country's shortcomings in rule or law remain a significant obstacle to further democratic consolidation. Indonesia successfully transitioned to democracy following the fall of Suharto in 1998. Incomplete institutional reforms, corruption and dysfunctional bureaucracy have been common features of the country's progress toward democratic consolidation. In 2002, Timor Leste became independent and joined the ranks of Asian democracies with much fanfare.

---

1 Freedom House. 2012 Freedom in the World Survey. www.Freedomhouse.org

The last decade, however, has seen slow progress and mixed results in both governance and democratization. Large shares of populations in Singapore and Malaysia have become vocal about the shortcoming of democracy in those countries, while remaining supportive of the authoritarian regimes that currently govern their countries. Finally, even if people in Thailand remain outspoken about the need for democracy to take firm roots in their country, Thailand "stop-and-go" process toward finding a legitimate form of government, with 18 constitutions and 18 coups since 1932, is without precedent in the annals of democracy.

Asia Struggles with Democracy investigates the role played by democratic knowledge, attitudes and behaviors of ordinary people in the democratization of Indonesia, Korea and Thailand. Many forces affect the emergence and stability of democracy such as elites interactions, economic development and popular attitudes. Beliefs and perceptions about the legitimacy of political systems have long been recognized as some of the most critical influences on regime change, and particularly on the consolidation or breakdown of democracy. Furthermore, normative commitment to democracy among the public at large is crucial for evaluating how far the political system has traveled toward democratic consolidation. Democratization can only happen if the majority of the people believes that democracy is the best form of government for their society while at the same time rejects any other form or government, particularly non democratic ones. This book explores what it is about the nature of public opinion and the processes of day-to-day democratic participation that have made Indonesia, Korea and Thailand vulnerable to repeated crises of legitimacy and seemingly lacking commitment toward democracy.

Asia Struggles with Democracy is informed by data from two original opinion surveys designed by the Southeast Asia Studies Program of the Paul H. Nitze School of Advanced International Studies (SAIS) of the Johns Hopkins University. The SAIS 2000 Survey was designed to investigate the 1997 East Asian financial crisis as a possible cause of broad social, economic and political changes that might alter the development trajectory of Indonesia, the Philippines, Korea and Thailand. The survey focused on the cities of Jakarta, Manila, Seoul and Bangkok, had a sampling size of 300 individuals per capital city and used a semi-original, 12-modules questionnaire, which comprised 135 questions, 10 percent of which were open-ended questions. The SAIS 2011 Survey is a national-level opinion survey, which targeted the same four countries of the SAIS 2000 Survey with a total sampling size of 4,000 individuals. To ensure consistency with the SAIS 2000 Survey, the 2011 survey included a capital-city sample of 300 individuals and an updated version of the questionnaire used for the 2000 survey.

The methodological challenge of establishing comparability in any cross-national survey remains formidable. The research compared national responses to questions that are identically worded but must be translated into a number of different languages and administered in different cultural and institutional contexts. Standardization does not solve the problem of cross-cultural validity, and the resulting analysis takes this issue under consideration by trying to strike a balance between generalizing cross-national comparisons and contextualizing the meaning and significance of data in their political and cultural settings. The SAIS Surveys are part of a new generation of comparative public survey projects such as the regional Barometer Surveys and the World Value Survey (WVS). Increasingly, these large surveys have cooperated with one another to standardize questions and response formats to achieve global comparability in understanding the third-wave transition to democracy and the role played by attitudes and values toward politics, governance, and political reforms. In this spirit, where possible, this book includes data from the WVS and the regional Barometer Surveys to validate and crosscheck the findings emerging from the SAIS Surveys.

The choice of Indonesia, Korea and Thailand as the focus of this book resulted from their institutional and political trajectories to become consolidated democracies and how their democratic choices might influence other countries in the region. When the SAIS 2000 Survey was launched in 2000, Indonesia, Korea and Thailand were democratic countries enduring the stresses created by the 1997–1998 East Asia financial crisis. At that time, Korea and Thailand appeared to be economically fragile but politically stable as power was transferred peacefully from one political group to another. Indonesia, in contrast, was just entering democratic transition and appeared on the brink of failure from the breakdown of law and order and the possibility of secession of various regions across the Indonesian archipelago. By the time the SAIS 2011 Survey entered the field, the list of relatively stable democracies in Asia had changed. It included Indonesia, along with Korea and the Philippines, while the democratic stature of Thailand had declined as a result of military and judicial coups that ousted democratically elected governments.

Korea's success in establishing democracy in a country without a democratic tradition has made it one of the most interesting cases of third-wave democratic transition. In the span of one generation, Korea has transforme itself from one of the poorest countries into one of the world's most succes ful economies. In the 1990s, Korea joined the Organisation for Econom Co-operation and Development (OECD), thus becoming the second cor try in Asia, after Japan, to join the OECD. Korea begun its transformat from military rule to representative democracy in the late 1980s, and o\

4 *Introduction*

10-year period, successfully established democratic institutions in a country that had not previously been capable of peacefully transferring power to the political opposition. In 1993, Kim Young-sam became the first civilian elected president in 30 years, and he has been succeeding in orderly elections featuring civilian politicians from different parties. There is consensus that a return to the pre-1993 days of military involvement in the political process has become virtually impossible. However, many scholars wonder how much progress Korea has made in consolidating its democracy, given that its presidents have at times resorted to extra-legal tactics to overcome the political deadlock in periods of divided governments, political parties are personal political vehicles and citizens' participation in day-to-day politics has been decreasing.

Indonesia is the latest democratization success story in Asia. As a result of the financial crisis of 1997–1998, President Suharto was driven from power through protests, the collapse of local and international private sector confidence and, most importantly, the decline of Suharto's support within the Jakarta elites. The future did not seem to augur well for democratic reform in the years immediately after Suharto's fall. Fragile governments faced emboldened legislatures, law and order declined for several years during the transfer of responsibility from the army to the police and loss of life occurred in ethno-religious conflicts. Yet, the drive for change that began during the 1997–1998 financial crisis was maintained through the dismissal of President Habibie, the impeachment of President Wahid and the lackluster administration of President Megawati. The fact that Indonesia made a successful democratic transition is not in dispute. Yet, the country's progress toward democratic consolidation might just not be as thorough as it seems. The political system has been showing signs of democratic stagnation and backsliding, with the political elites trying to tighten its grip on key institutions, often in ways that reduce transparency and the effectiveness of the institutions themselves. In addition, parliamentary and party systems are becoming increasingly associated with lack of accountability and discretion and citizens' confidence in the strength of the democratic consolidation in Indonesia appears to have decreased over time.

Finally, the checkered relationship between Thailand and democracy is without precedent in democratic history. In 1932, a bloodless coup by a group of elite military and elite bureaucrats replaced an absolute constitutional monarchy. Democracy, however, remained elusive and government in Thailand continued to be an exchange of power among various entourages of the Thai elite. Between 1932 and 1991, military coups rather than general elections were the normal means of changing governments, with elections held only to legitimize the new arrangements domestically and internationally. Democratically elected governments, including that of media tycoon turned political leader, Thaksin Shinawatra, ruled Thailand from 1992–2006. Thaksin's government had been preceded by a series of weak, multi-party governments that were dominated by up-country, often corrupt politicians whom the Bangkok elites despised. Through his personal fortune and populist policies that shifted benefits to his constituents in the North and Northeast provinces, Thaksin Shinawatra built the first popular political party in Thailand. Prime Minister Thaksin's charismatic hold upon his supporters remained strong even after he was deposed by a military coup in 2006. His political parties, even after being disbanded by court decisions, continued to outpace all others in the 2007, 2011 and 2014 national elections. Thailand seems to be caught between a traditional elite-centric, administrative state and democratic mass public participation. Because of this, Thailand is never more than just a step away from constantly falling back into authoritarianism.

The findings from the SAIS 2000 and 2011 Surveys presented in this book show the relevance of mass attitudes for democratic consolidation across Indonesia, Korea and Thailand, where citizens seem to be favorably disposed toward democracy, but not necessarily committed to it. Across the three countries, democracy is understood and well valued as an idea or a set of values. However, as a regime to be chosen as the preferred way to govern any of these countries, democracy does not seem as popular and seems to still have to prove itself through successful and consistent performance. Equally relevant the fact that in Indonesia, Korea and Thailand concepts such as non-electoral participation, membership and participation in civil society organizations, economics or the middle class do not play as relevant a role as argued by democratic theory and showed by the success of Western Liberal democratic tradition.

The chapters of this book are unified by the survey questions that inform them. This uniformity makes cross-national comparisons possible while allowing for contextualized interpretations of the findings, with chapters applying expert knowledge of each country democratization path, evolving institutional setting, changing social and economic conditions and national political dynamics. Chapter 1 introduces the book to the reader. Chapter 2 examines citizens' cognitive orientations toward democracy – that is, what democracy means, or what they expected it to be – in Indonesia, Korea and Thailand, tries to identify relevant trends across the three countries as well as those unique to each country. It considers whether citizens' conceptions of democracy are based either on enduring cultural values, social circumstances, or the degree of their formal and informal political participation. Finally, findings from comparative research on the meaning of democracy, based on data from the WVS and the Barometer Surveys, are weaved into the narrative to check whether the findings for Indonesia, Korea and

Thailand from the SAIS 2000 and 2011 Surveys are consistent with those of other countries in Asia and around the world.

Citizens' understanding of democracy is important as it provides information about what people may want from democracy, which in turn influences how satisfied citizens might be about democracy in general and in their own countries. Democracy is "probably the most complex concept in political sciences"[2] which is embraced by both democratic and non-democratic regimes thanks to its positive connotations. Large majorities of people in authoritarian societies like China, Vietnam and Singapore are satisfied with democracy in their countries, often to a degree higher than that of consolidated democracies like Japan or Taiwan. This reality, on the one hand, suggests the existence of a wide variety of democratic conceptions that act as lenses through which people evaluate democracy in their own countries and eventually embrace it exclusively and fully. On the other hand, it questions whether citizens' conceptions are the bases for democratic cultures to develop and strengthen. Chapter 2 shows that citizens in Indonesia, Korea and Thailand are cognitively capable of defining democracy, that particular aspects of modernization theory are helpful to explain what shapes citizens' democratic cognitive skills across the three countries, and that what citizens learn from what democracy is and what it does at home shapes their overall views about democracy as a political system but not as a value itself.

Chapter 3 unpacks the specific terms in which ordinary citizens in Indonesia, Korea and Thailand understand democracy. The chapter analyzes the content of citizens' responses to the open-ended question "What does democracy mean to you?" to capture what elements of democracy Indonesians, Koreans and Thais consider the most or least essential, whether they impute positive or negative meanings to democracy and understand it in procedural or substantive terms. The study of cognitive orientations as related to political systems is not new, and differences in the understanding of democracy among citizens have been implicitly assumed by many scholars. Yet, as the operationalization and measurement of concepts, as well as sufficient historical and comparative data to test the key linkages have proved largely elusive, the systematic analysis of the content of citizens' cognitive orientations and its relationship with affective and evaluative support for political systems has been limited. The chapter shows that the majority of polled citizens has a positive, multi-dimensional view of democracy, and that Indonesians and Koreans see democracy as a political system where its intended outcomes – freedom, liberty and rights – are more

---

2 Michael Coppedge. 2002. "Democracy and Dimensions. Comments on Munck and Verkuilen". Comparative Political Studies. Vol. 35, No. 1, pp. 35–39.

important than how the democratic processes work, whereas Thais seem to think that electoral and constitutional procedures are enough to guarantee democracy in Thailand. Understanding the elements of democracy that ordinary citizens consider the most and least essential for the development of democracy in their own countries provides a framework to gauge their democratic aspirations, with each interpretation having different implications for the principles and norms underpinning each country's democratic cultures and how democracy consolidates in Indonesia, Korea and Thailand. As in Chapter 2, findings from existing comparative research from the WVS and the Barometer Surveys are weaved into the chapter narrative to show whether the findings for Indonesia, Korea and Thailand from the SAIS 2000 and 2011 Surveys are consistent with those of other countries in Asia and/or around the world.

Chapter 4 discusses citizens' knowledge of Asian democratic and authoritarian regimes in Indonesia, Korea and Thailand, and presents the findings from existing and new spatial econometric analysis (based on data from the Polity IV Project) regarding the spread of democracy worldwide and across Asia. A known theme in democratic literature argues that one country's political and institutional choices could be influenced by forces originating outside a country's borders – rather than being a self-contained domestic process – and proposes various interpretations of how democratization occurs and what role citizens play in this process. This idea is interesting but not new, as Emanuel Kant already suggested that the causes of democracy could be found beyond a country's borders in the 18th century. More recently, Rustow, Whitehead, Hungtington and Starr have referred to this theory to help explain the diffusion of democratic processes around the world. The chapter shows that across Indonesia, Korea and Thailand the vast majority of citizens are sure that their country is a democracy. Yet, they are rather unsure of whether countries in Asia such as China, India and the Philippines are democratic or authoritarian, with knowledge of democratic political systems in the region being poorer than that of authoritarian countries. Moreover, findings from the spatial econometric analysis show that while democratic diffusion happens both worldwide and across Asia, the annual rates of diffusion indicate that the strength with which democracy spread across countries might have been generally overstated.

Chapter 5 discusses what motivates ordinary citizens to embrace democracy as the preferred system of government by investigating citizens' affective support for authoritarian or democratic political systems in Indonesia, Korea and Thailand. If the daily news is to be believed, it seems that most people around the world, and in Asia, want democracy. Yet, existing assessments on the levels of support for democracy have been severely criticized in recent years, as for democracy to take firm roots, it requires that large majorities of citizens consider democracy their preferred political regime, while rejecting any non-democratic alternatives. Citizens with little experience of and limited sophistication concerning democratic politics may be uncertain whether democracy or authoritarianism offers the best solution to the problems facing their countries and often end up embracing both democracy and authoritarianism at the same time. Moreover, affective support for democracy can be temporary or weak and lead to temporal instability for Gibson's apt description of the democratic reality in the former Soviet Union where "support for democracy could be a mile wide and an inch deep",[3] which makes it difficult for "democracy to be the only game in town".[4] The chapter finds that in Indonesia, Korea and Thailand the consistency and depth of support for democracy as "the only game in town" is shallow at best. At one level, democracy represents a clear set of political values to which citizens aspire. At another level, however, democracy refers to a political regime-in-practice that citizens might or might not want as the system by which their countries are governed, thus revealing a significant gulf between these two levels of democratic support at the mass level. Moreover, authoritarian affective support emerges as appealing as, and at times stronger than, democratic affective support in spite of their citizens' positive views of democracy.

Chapter 6 closes the book and discusses the findings and trends that have been observed across the mass citizenries in Indonesia, Korea and Thailand in the context of democratization trends around the world. Chapter 6 shows how unique each country's and the region's paths to democracy are when compared to those of other regions, and particularly those of Western liberal democracies, and concludes that a substantial length of the road must still be travelled before democracy becomes fully consolidated across Indonesia, Korea and Thailand.

---

3   James L. Gibson. 1996. "A Mile Wide But an Inch Deep (?): The Structure of Democratic Commitments in the Former USSR". American Journal of Political Science. Vol. 40, No. 2, pp. 396–420.
4   Larry Diamond. 1999. Developing Democracy: Toward Consolidation. Baltimore, MD: Johns Hopkins University Press.
    Juan J. Linz and Alfred Stepan. 1996. Problems of Democratic Transition and Consolidation: Southern Europe, South America, and Post-Communist Europe. Baltimore, MD: Johns Hopkins University Press.
    Doh Chull Shin. 2007. "Democratization: Perspectives from Global Citizenry". The Oxford Handbook of Political Behavior, edited by Russel Dalton and Hans-Dieter Klingemann. New York, NY: Oxford University Press.

2 What does democracy mean to you?

Democracy is "probably the most complex concept in political sciences"[1] which is embraced by both democratic and non-democratic regimes thanks to its positive connotations. Large majorities of people in authoritarian societies like China, Vietnam and Singapore are satisfied with democracy in their countries, often to a degree that outranks that of consolidated democracies like Japan or Taiwan. This reality suggests the existence of a wide variety of democratic conceptions that act as lenses through which people understand and evaluate democracy in their own countries and eventually embrace it exclusively and fully as the type of regime to govern their country. This chapter examines mass citizenries' cognitive orientations toward democracy – that is, what democracy is, or what they expected it to be. Learning about citizens' understanding of democracy is important as it provides information about what people might want from democracy, which in turn could influence citizens' satisfaction with democracy in general, and in their own countries more specifically.

The study of public opinion on democracy is not new. Yet, more often than not, it has assumed that people know relatively little about democracy and that, regardless of how much they might know, a shared understanding of democracy among the people is likely to exist. This chapter argues that citizens do know what democracy is, even if their knowledge might vary according to political sophistication, and that they do not necessarily understand democracy in the same way. Then, this chapter investigates whether citizens' conception of democracy are based either on enduring cultural values, or social circumstances, or the degree of their formal and informal political participation, or participation in civic and religious

---

1 Michael Coppedge. 2002. "Democracy and Dimensions. Comments on Munck and Verkuilen". Comparative Political Studies. Vol. 35, No. 1, pp. 35–39.

organizations, or upon what they learn from short-, medium- and long-term experience about what democracy is and what it does both at home and abroad. Finally, findings from comparative research on the meaning of democracy, based on data from the World Value Survey (WVS) and the Barometer Surveys, are weaved into the chapter narrative to show whether the findings for Indonesia, Korea and Thailand from the SAIS 2011 Survey are consistent with those of other countries in Asia and around the world.

A recurrent problem in the study of citizens' democratic cognitive skills is finding adequate data and to establish whether available items can be used to operationalize this concepts. The 2011 SAIS Survey[2] asked an open-ended question of a cognitive nature[3] – "What does democracy mean to you?" – to investigate whether Indonesian, Korean and Thai citizens could define democracy in their own words and identify its most essential properties. Across the three countries, responses included a wide array of statements, including the following:

> *democracy means having popular sovereignty", or "democracy means that there is no possibility of a prolonged one-man rule", or "democracy means a government which reflects the opinions of ordinary people and not only those of the elites", or "democracy means that a country is not ruled by military power", or "democracy means freedom to express opinions on leaders", or "democracy means that a country follows a proper change of government", or "democracy means that the country is not a dictatorship", or "democracy means that people participate in governing the country.*

2 Refer to Annex 1 for background on the 2000 and 2011 SAIS Surveys.
3 To examine the meanings that citizens associate with democracy, current scholarship relies on different strategies. Open-ended survey questions help identify any meanings attached to the democracy word, whereas respondents' choices out of pre-selected attributes identify the most essential characteristics of democracy to gauge their democratic conceptions. Both strategies have their own advantages and disadvantages to minimize the bias caused by questionnaire design. The open-ended question provides sufficient flexibility and freedom for respondents and collects all possible responses. Yet, it is difficult to implement, and the findings are conditional upon the coding schemes used for analysis. Close-ended survey instruments with pre-selected answer categories ease the implementation, reduce the subjective bias in data analysis and facilitate cross-regional comparative research; however, there is scholarly agreement that pre-selected answer categories significantly shape and constrain respondents' possible answers.

Overall, responses to the open-ended question show that citizens in Indonesia, Korea and Thailand are able to define democracy in their own words and think of democracy in significant different ways even if, generally speaking, they understand democracy as a competitive system of governance in which people have a dispositive say in how they are governed. This is an important finding because people's understanding of democracy is likely to determine their ideas about the development of democratic principles through norms and structures, and ultimately what they expect these norms and structures to deliver. Moreover, only if democracy as an idea is meaningful to citizens (i.e. they know what it is), they can eventually express affective and/or evaluative support for it as a form of government.

Thailand is the country where the largest share of respondents offered their definitions of democracy (i.e. 90 percent) followed by Indonesia (i.e. 86 percent) and Korea (i.e. 80 percent). Perhaps, it is not surprising to see that democracy is such a popular concept among citizens in Thailand and Indonesia, although the reasons for these two countries to be top ranking are different and telling of two different democratic political cultures. Indonesia is the latest country in Asia to have made a successful transition to democracy[4] following the fall a President Suharto in May 1998. Since then, it has made progress toward democratic consolidation,[5] even if progress has been uneven across institutional areas. The transformed political context is very likely to have played a role in sharpening Indonesians' cognitive awareness of democracy. Thailand's tradition of recurrent coups d'état, new

---

4 Democratic theory identifies democratic transition as the initial movement away from an authoritarian system during which there is a replacement of the non-democratic institutions and procedures. Necessary aspects of this transition are the implementation of new rules governing the political process and an initial willingness on the part of political actors to follow these newly established rules. According to democratic theory, transition ends with the first democratic elections and the assumption of power by the democratically elected government. For more on democratic transition see: O'Donnell Guillermo, Schmitter Philippe and Lawrence Whitehead (Eds.). Transition from Authoritarian Rule: Prospects for Democracy, Baltimore, MD: Johns Hopkins University Press.

5 Democratic consolidation is the more complex phase of the democratization process; it generally involves the process of making the new democratic institutions and procedures a routine part of the political process within the country. During this phase, the adaptation of the new rules and procedures leads to a persistence of process and a stable democratic system. Not surprisingly, the more open-ended nature of this phase has also led to a much wider diversity in the way it is characterized in the literature.

constitutions and urban political elites meddling with the political process has given the country one of the most checkered democratic history in Asia which, in turn, might have heightened Thais' democratic cognitive skills. Finally, Korea is considered one of the most successful examples of third wave democracies,[6] and yet democracy emerges as slightly less popular than in Indonesia and Thailand. This finding might be suggestive of a more mature democratic culture where citizens' democratic cognitive skills are subtler than in other countries. However, it could also be symptomatic of limited progress made in the democratization of the country's institutions and the political and cultural values that used to support Korea's military leadership.

Comparative research, based on data from the Barometer surveys,[7] suggests that citizens' ability to conceptualize democracy in Indonesia, Korea and Thailand is consistent with that of citizens in other countries around the world. The Barometer Surveys for Russia and Ukraine, for the early 1990s, show that three-quarters of citizens across the two countries were able to define democracy, thus confirming the salience of democracy as a concept in times of institutional and political transition.[8] In

---

6 Third wave democracy refers to the third major surge of democracy in history. Samuel P. Huntington coined the term in his 1991 book *The Third Wave: Democratization in the Late Twentieth Century*. Huntington describes global democratization as coming in waves; the first wave of democracy began in the early 19th century when suffrage was granted to the majority of white males in the United States. At its peak, the first wave saw 29 democracies in the world. This continued until 1922, when Benito Mussolini rose to power in Italy. The ebb of the first wave lasted from 1922 until 1942, during which the number of democracies in the world dropped to a mere 12. The second wave began following the Allied victory in World War II and crested nearly 20 years later in 1962 with 36 recognized democracies in the world. The second wave ebbed at this point, and the total number dropped to 30 democracies between 1962 and the mid-1970s. The third wave began its upward climb in 1974, doubling the number of democracies in just a few decades. Today, there are some 60 democracies in the world, the most to date. Many political scientists and theorists believe that in accordance with history, this third wave has crested and will soon ebb just as its predecessors did. Huntington agreed that these predictions are certainly possible; however, no such events can truly be predicted, even with years of history as a model.

7 The Barometer Surveys are comparative surveys of attitudes and values toward politics, power, reform, democracy and citizens' political actions in 55 political systems across Africa, Asia, Latin America and the Arab region.

8 Arthur H Miller, Vicki Miller and William Reisinger. 1997. "Conceptions of Democracy Among Mass and Elite in Post-Soviet Societies". British Journal of Political Science. Vol. 27, No. 2, pp. 157–190.

other post-communist countries, those who gave a definition of democracy ranged from a low 66 percent in Romania to a high 87 percent in the Czech Republic during the same years. In the early 2000s, the Afrobarometer surveys[9] found greater variation in the shares of respondents offering their conceptions of democracy in African countries than those observed in Indonesia, Korea and Thailand. Citizens who were able to define democracy ranged from a low of 58 percent in Lesotho to a high of 98 percent in Nigeria. Finally, the Asian Barometer surveys[10] show rates ranging from a high 90 percent in Singapore and 83 percent in Vietnam, to a low 69 percent in the Philippines and 68 percent in Malaysia between 2005 and 2007.

Discriminant analysis[11] shows that across the three countries, citizens who offered their definition of democracy are a group distinct from those who declined to do so by their urban status, older age, higher levels of education, participation in both electoral and non-electoral activities and knowledge of Asian political systems. The differences between the two groups, however, are not particularly significant, thus suggesting that citizens who did not share their conception of democracy might be citizens who are simply reluctant to share their views in public opinion surveys, and not necessarily citizens who are not capable of defining democracy. Moreover, while there is no specific literature on the reasons why people think of democracy differently, limited scholarly work has focused on the factors – e.g. demographics, socio-economics, political and cultural ones – which influence citizens' democratic cognitive skills around the world. Analytical evidence emerging from the SAIS 2011 Survey suggest that factors influencing citizens' democratic cognitive skills in Indonesia, Korea and Thailand are largely country specific, and their overlap across the three countries is limited to i) citizens'

---

9 Michael Bratton, Robert Mattes and E. Gyimah-Boadi. 2004. Public Opinion, Democracy, and Market Reform in Africa. Cambridge, UK: Cambridge University Press.
10 Jie Lu. 2012. "Democratic Conceptions in East Asian Societies: A Contextualized Analysis". Paper prepared for the conference on "How the Public Views Democracy and Its Competitors in East Asia: Taiwan in Comparative Perspective". Stanford University, Stanford, May 25–26, 2012.
   Larry Diamond Jay and Marc F. Plattner. 2008. How People View Democracy. Baltimore, MD: Johns Hopkins University Press.
11 Linear discriminant analysis is used in statistics to find combinations of features that characterize or separate two or more classes of people, objects, or events.

14 *What does democracy mean to you?*

knowledge of their countries' governance structures[12] and ii) consumption of consumer goods.[13]

---

12 Questions 82 and 83 of the SAIS 2011 Survey inquire about the political institutional structure of Indonesia, Korea and Thailand. Specifically, Question 82 asks, What is the most important political institution for (insert country name)? (SA) R1. President (or Prime Minister for Thailand); R2. National parliament; R3. Judiciary; R4. Political parties; R5. Local governments; R6. Do not know. The rationale for including this question in the SAIS 2011 Survey was to understand whether citizens in Indonesia, Korea and Thailand know what are the key institutions and their functions in their respective countries, regardless of their perception of the importance and relevance of national- or local-level institutions.

Question 83 asks the following: At present, which political institution, if any, needs to be improved? R1. President (or Prime Minister for Thailand); R2. National parliament; R3. Judiciary; R4. Political parties; R5. Local governments; R6. Others, specify; R7. None needs to be changed; R8. Do not know. This question was meant to inquire about citizens' understanding of existing shortcoming in the processes and functioning of their country's political institutions at national and local level.

13 Question 43 of the SAIS 2011 Survey inquires about consumption of consumer goods. Specifically, Question 43 asks: Now I am going to ask you some questions about what you or your household consume. Compared to three years ago, how would you describe the amount of each product your household is currently consuming: 1. Beef; R1. More; R2. Just as much; R3. Less; R4. Have stopped consuming/buying; R5. Never bought; R6. Do not know. 2. Vegetables; R1. More; R2. Just as much; R3. Less; R4. Have stopped consuming/buying; R5. Never bought; R6. Do not know. 3. Soft drinks; R1. More; R2. Just as much; R3. Less; R4 .Have stopped consuming/buying; R5. Never bought; R6. Do not know. 4. Clothes and shoes; R1. More; R2. Just as much; R3. Less; R4. Have stopped consuming/buying; R5. Never bought; R6. Do not know.

Based on the individual responses to Question 43, a Consumption Scale has been constructed. The four items included (i.e. beef, vegetable, soft drinks, clothes and shoes) were subjected to factor and principal component analysis. The Kaiser-Meyer-Oklin value was of .637, and the principal component analysis revealed the presence of two components with eigenvalues exceeding 1, which together explained the 68.9 percent of the total variance. Consumption of beef, soft drinks and clothes and shoes loads on one factor, whereas consumption of vegetables moves in the opposite direction and loads on a second, different factor. The Catell's scree test indicated that only one component should be retained for further investigation, thus suggesting that the variable for consumption of vegetables should be excluded from the Consumption Scale for each of the three countries. The Consumption Scale comprises five levels to allow for an approximate variance of 20 percent between levels; the five levels of the scale are: i) "More or Just About the Same", which identifies respondents whose consumption patterns of beef, soft drinks, clothes and shoes has either increased or stayed the same, over the last three years; ii) "Mixed", which identified respondents whose consumption patterns of either beef, or soft drinks, clothes and shoes could have increased or decreased, thus resulting in an overall mixed consumption trend, over the last three years; iii) "Declining", which identifies respondents whose consumption patterns of beef, soft drinks, clothes and shoes has followed a consistent declining trend, over the last three years; iv) "Severely Declining", which identifies respondents whose consumption of beef, soft drinks, clothes and shoes has declined significantly over the last three years; v) "Stopped Buying or Never Bought", which identifies respondents who stopped consuming beef, soft drinks, clothes and shoes, or never bought any of these three goods over the last three years.

Sartori,[14] Lijphart,[15] Linz,[16] and Reilly[17] have argued that political engineering (i.e. design and structure institutions to achieve a particular objective) can help strengthen or limit democracy, and while there is agreement that institutions matter to political development, there remains disagreement about which institutional structures are the most likely to support and strengthen democracy in diverse societies. As citizens' idea of democracy is influenced – implicitly or explicitly – by what democracy does or does not do in their own countries, it is an important finding that citizens' knowledge of their countries' institutional and political architectures has an influence on their democratic cognitive skills.

Equally important is the relevance of micro-level economics (such as individual consumption of consumer goods) as one of the key factors influencing citizens' ability to define democracy. Lerner,[18] Lipset,[19] and Inkeles[20] have long argued that economic development leads to democracy. Przeworski[21] and Lewis-Beck[22] have provided evidence that economic development contributes to democracy. More recently, using quantitative evidence from the former Soviet Union and Eastern European countries, Duch[23] and Gibson[24] have shown that economic stability is as important as economic development in influencing how citizens conceive democracy.

---

14 Giovanni Sartori. 1968. "Political Development and Political Engineering". Public Policy, Vol. 17, pp. 261–298.
15 Arend Lijphart and Bernanrd Grofman (Eds.). 1984. Choosing an Electoral System: Issues and Alternatives. New York, NY: Praeger.
16 Juan Linz. 1990. "The Perils of Presidentialism". Journal of Democracy. Vol. 1, No. 1, pp. 51–69.
17 Benjamin Reilly. 2006. Democracy and Diversity: Political Engineering in the Asia-Pacific. New York, NY: Oxford University Press.
18 Daniel Lerner. 1958. The Passing of Traditional Society. New York, NY: Free Press of Glencoe.
19 Seymour Martin Lipset. 1963. Political Man: The Social Bases of Politics. New York, NY: Anchor Books.
20 Alex Inkeles and David H. Smith. 1974. Becoming Modern: Individual Change in Six Developing Countries. Cambridge, MA: Harvard University Press.
21 Adam Przeworski and Fernando Limongi. 1997. "Modernization: Theories and Facts." World Politics. Vol. 49, No. 2, pp. 155–183.
22 Michael S. Lewis-Beck. 1988. Economics and Elections: The Major Western Democracies. Ann Arbor: University of Michigan Press.
23 Raymond M. Duch. 1993. "Tolerating Economic Reform: Popular Support for Transition to a Free Market in Republics of the Former Soviet Union". American Political Science Review. Vol. 87, No. 3, pp. 590–608.
24 James L. Gibson. 1996. "A Mile Wide But an Inch Deep(?): The Structure of Democratic Commitments in the Former USSR", American Journal of Political Science. Vol. 40, No. 2, pp. 396–420.

16 *What does democracy mean to you?*

In Indonesia, factors influencing citizens' democratic cognitive skills range from knowledge of the country's political governance structure, to individual consumption of consumer goods, to age and gender, and urban and rural status.[25] Some 52 percent of Indonesians identified the presidency as Indonesia's most important institution, thus indicating that the just about half of the population of Indonesia know that their country is a presidential democracy where citizens directly elect their president. This finding is surprising because with the exception of the years between 1950 and 1957, which saw a short-lived attempt at a Dutch-style parliamentary democracy – known as Demokrasi Liberal – Indonesia has always been a presidential system. Yet, the way presidentialism has played out in Indonesia could offer some insights of why barely more than half of the population appears to be knowledgeable about the relevance of the presidency vis-à-vis other political institutions. The years of Demokrasi Liberal were an extended period of political instability, characterized by religious, cultural and regional based conflict. The economy was in a disastrous state following almost 10 years of Japanese occupation and war against the Dutch, and young and inexperienced governments were unable to boost production of food and other necessities to keep pace with a fast paced population growth. Inflation was rampant, smuggling cost the central government much needed foreign exchange and much of the plantations had been destroyed during the occupation and war. Furthermore, a proliferation of political parties and the deals brokered between them for cabinet seats resulted in political gridlock and rapid turnover of government coalitions. Parliament-style democracy ended with the imposition of martial law and President Sukarno's introduction of Guided Democracy in 1957,[26] during which Indonesia became more autocratic and the power of the presidency was strongly reasserted. Presidential power, in fact, was radically centralized under the framework of the New Order,[27] and no effective institutional checks

---

25 Question 10 of the SAIS 2011 Survey inquires about respondents' locale of residence. Specifically, Question 10 asks, Where do you reside? (SA) R1. Urban, capital city; R2. Urban, non-capital city; R3. Rural.
26 Guided Democracy (GD) was the brainchild of President Sukarno and represented an attempt to bring about political stability following the years of Demokrasi Liberal. It lasted from 1957 until 1966 when Suharto's New Order began. GD was based on the traditional village system of discussion and consensus under the guidance of village elders. The centerpiece would be a mutual cooperation cabinet of the major parties advised by a National Council of functional groups, with a threefold blend of nationalism, religion and communism into a co-operative government. This was intended to appease the three main factions in Indonesian politics – the army, Islamic groups and the Communists.
27 The New Order is the term coined by President Suharto to characterize his regime, as he came to power in 1966, and contrast his rule with that of his predecessor, Sukarno. Following Suharto's fall in 1998, the term New Order has become synonymous with Suharto's leadership.

and balances on presidential legislative power were set in place in spite of the 1945 Constitution stating that presidential power was "not unlimited", that "the president was to be subordinated and accountable to the Majelis Permusyawaratan Rakyat (MPR)",[28] and that "the MPR had the right to dismiss the president before the end of his or her term in the event of clear violation of national policy (which included the 1945 Constitution and the content and the Broad Guidelines of State Policy)."[29] The limitations applied to presidential power between 1999 and 2001 during the first wave of post-Suharto democratic reforms, and the removal of President Wahid[30] from office in 2001 showed that, if followed, the procedures dictated by the 1945 Constitution could have real teeth. The flipside of these procedures in a time of legislative assertiveness was that the president had to bargain over legislation with a highly fragmented legislature and could achieve very little. Since 2001, various rounds of constitutional reforms have led to further change. The principle that the sovereignty of the people was to be exercised directly and not through the MPR was set in place. This led to establishment of the fundamental structure of the presidential system based on the principles of separation of powers, direct presidential election and impeachment of the president and

---

28 The Majelis Permusyawaratan Rakyat (i.e. the People's Consultative Assembly of the Republic of Indonesia) is the legislative branch of Indonesia's political system. It is composed of the members of the People's Representative Council and of the Regional Representative Council. Before 2004 and the amendments to the 1945 Constitution, MPR was the highest governing body in Indonesia. In accordance with Law No. 16/1960, the assembly was formed after the first general election of 1971. It was decided at that time that the membership of the MPR would be twice that of the Representative House. The 920 membership of MPR continued for the periods of 1977–1982 and 1982–1987. For the periods 1987–1992, 1992–1997 and 1997–1999, the MPR's membership became 1000. One hundred members were appointed representing delegations from groups as addition to the factions' delegates of Karya Pembangunan, Partai Demokrasi Indonesia and Persatuan Pembangunan. For the period of 1999–2004, the membership of MPR was only 700, likewise for the 2004–2009 period.

29 Section 6 of the elucidation to the 1945 Constitution.

30 In 1999, Abdurrahman Wahid emerged as the first democratically elected president of Indonesia. He had been head of the small but high-profile Democracy Forum set up to oppose President Suharto's authoritarian rule. He came to the presidency with a reputation of a democrat, the leader of Indonesia largest traditionalist Islamic organization, strongly committed to inter-faith dialogue and a staunch opponent of Islamic fundamentalism. Yet, President Wahid's 35-member Cabinet lacked political coherence, mostly because the posts were divided among the parties based on their contribution to the President Wahid's election. By the end of his first year in office in October 2000, he had alienated virtually all the parties that had voted for him in 1999, and his casual use of government and state funding made him vulnerable to parliamentary retaliation. The Bulog-gate and the Brunei-gate scandals gave the president's opponents in the DPR the grounds they needed to commence the impeachment proceedings against him, which ended in July 2001 with both President Wahid's and his vice president's dismissals.

the vice-president for constitutional breach, and not on policy or confidence grounds, and the adoption of presidential terms limits. Compared to the recent past, the presidency was set to enjoy a strengthened and more balanced position vis-à-vis the legislature.

The remaining 48 percent of Indonesians seems to be less clear about their country political institutional structure. In fact, 24 percent believe that the national parliament is the most important institution; another 10 percent think it is the local governments, whereas 9 percent of Indonesians give primacy to the judiciary and 2 percent to political parties. Finally, 3 percent of polled citizens declined to answer. So many incorrect views regarding Indonesia's governance structure could be the result of the many institutional changes and reforms that have taken place following the 1998 fall of President Suharto, with the most thorough reforms targeting governing institutions. Incorrect views could be the legacy of both the pre-2004 presidential system and the impact of the country's Big Bang Decentralization, which transformed Indonesia in one of the most decentralized countries in the world. The enactment of Law No 22/1999 on Local Autonomy and Law No.25 on Financial Balance between the Central and Local Governments in 2001 marked the watershed in the central-local political relationships. These new laws resulted in the bureaucracy being restructured to deliver services at the local level; to allow the elections of governors, district heads and mayors to be representatives of their own constituencies rather than appointees of the central government in Jakarta; and to guarantee local governments the allocation of a certain level of finances to fulfill their autonomous functions. Regional governments acquired more control over their own affairs than during President Suharto's New Order, although the performance of the majority of them often failed to meet the standards of good governance. The 2000 Regional Autonomy Law was replaced by a new Regional Autonomy Law in 2004. While the 2000 Law had caused significant confusion, the primary reason for its replacement, was the fact that the central government wished to regain some of the power it had relinquished to cities and districts following the implementation of the Big Bang Decentralization in 2001. The Autonomy Law of 2004 achieved this by giving greater lawmaking powers to provinces and making provincial governors official central government representatives responsible to the President rather than to their constituencies. The 2000 Law had given only limited lawmaking and other powers to provincial governments. In other words, provinces were not "naturally" superior to districts and cities. Provinces were largely confined to mediating disputes between districts, facilitating cross-district development and representing the central government within the province. Instead, Article 382(1) of the 2004 Autonomy Law empowered governors to "guide and supervise governance in districts and cities" and to "coordinate the implementation of central government affairs in provinces, districts and cities". This meant that through governors, the central Indonesian government, primarily the Ministry for Home Affairs, could theoretically retain control over sub-provincial policy and lawmaking. To date, only few local governments seem to have succeeded at shaping local policy that is innovative and isolated from (inevitable) short-terms demands, and to create horizontal networks of supporters to institutionalize these processes.

More than a decade of institutional changes notwithstanding, the reality of a 52/48 ratio between Indonesians who are and are not knowledgeable about their country's political structure is not a positive finding, with the potential for negative impacts on both Indonesia democratic consolidation and the strengthening of its democratic culture.

As for the institution that needs the most reform, 23 percent of Indonesians think that it is the judiciary, whereas 22 percent that it is the parliament. Moreover, 10 percent of respondents believe that the status quo should be maintained, thus suggesting that for 24 million Indonesians the current structure and functioning of the country's governance setting does not have any particular problems. Finally, 9 percent of polled citizens declined to answer. These results confirm the long-standing, notorious reputation of the Indonesian judiciary at the mass level,[31] and possibly more worrisome, the fact that the least of progress in the country's comprehensive institutional reform program – which started in 1999 – has been made in the judicial sector. When President Suharto resigned his presidency in 1998, one of the loudest and most insistent demands was for legal reform, which meant nothing less than guaranteeing an honest, consistent and predictable legal process. This was hardly anything new. Demands for the judiciary to be restored were loud but had been consistently ignored by Indonesia's political elites. For a brief time after the fall of Suharto, hopes for legal reform seemed optimistic as the attention from local and international press made the needed reforms seem inevitable. Pressure was directed at the courts, prosecution, police, the legal profession, parliament and the Ministry of Justice. New commercial courts were established and a newly appointed National Law Commission began addressing basic issues of reforms. However, as President Habibie was replaced by President Wahid, who was forced from office and succeeded by President Megawati, optimism for reforms started to visibly fade. It is not as nothing useful has happened. Yet, the glacial pace at which anything has and continues to happen makes it difficult to convince the Indonesian public that a meaningful transformation of the judiciary is taking place. For

---

31 Sebastian Pompe. 2005. A Study of Institutional Collapse. Southeast Asia Program Publications. Ithaca, NY: Cornell University Press.

citizens, judicial institutions, more than any other institution, tend to define the quality of their state, their political system and leadership. When judicial institutions work well, they enjoy respect; when they fail, authority disappears in favor of power. This provokes people's anger and contempt, which seems all that most Indonesians feel about their judiciary.

Discriminant analysis shows that the Indonesians who would like a better judiciary and a better parliament are also those who think that the presidency is the country's most important institution whereas those who think that Indonesia's governance structure does not need any improvement belong to the 48 percent of citizens with limited knowledge of the country's political institutional structure. Regression modeling shows that Indonesians who think that the judiciary or the parliament are the institutions most in need of reform are respectively eight and five times more likely to have democratic cognitive skills than Indonesians that think that the institutional status quo should be maintained. Understanding what political institutions need to be improved shows that Indonesians are clear on what institutions are important for democracy to deliver on its promises, and both the inadequacies and virtues of their country institutional democratic processes. Regression modeling does not offer any meaningful insights regarding the relevance of knowledge of Indonesia most important political institution vis-à-vis citizens' democratic cognitive skills. However, it shows that knowledge of what parts of the country's governance structure need improvement does influence citizens' democratic cognitive skills. This finding is relevant because tells that the institutions that citizens recognize as low quality or malfunctioning impact how they understand democracy.

Changes in disposable income are important for how Indonesians define democracy. Data show that between 2009 and 2011, consumption levels "increased or stayed the same" for 25 percent of Indonesians. An average 15 to 17 percent of citizens experienced a "severe decline" in consumption patterns, whereas 22 percent saw dramatic negative changes in their disposable income (i.e. "stopped buying or never bought items like beef, soft drinks, clothes and shoes"). Regression modeling shows that those among the poorest in consumption terms are four times more likely to have democratic cognitive skills than citizens whose declines in disposable income have been less severe, or those who have not experienced any changes in consumption. This is an important finding as it signals that how citizens define democracy is not vulnerable to changes in their personal economic well-being. Moreover, it suggests that for most Indonesians, the idea of democracy does not necessarily hinge on a political system being able to deliver on economic growth. This finding is broadly consistent with what was seen in the former Soviet Union for the period 1989–1996.

As for the remaining factors influencing how Indonesians define democracy, being a resident of Jakarta makes a difference. In fact, those who reside in the capital are 6.5 times more likely to have a conception of democracy than Indonesians who reside in secondary cities or rural areas. This finding is important for various reasons; first, because the majority of Indonesians do not reside in Jakarta but either in urban areas other than Jakarta (i.e. 43 percent) or in rural areas (i.e. 39 percent).[32] Second, because Jakarta used to be the primary locale of the anti-Suharto movement and thus likely to have a higher level of civic literacy than the rest of the country; third, the strong "Jakarta effect" suggests that having democratic cognitive skills is not an effect of urbanization, but solely the effect of living in the Indonesian capital. Finally, this finding could be a sign of the fact that Indonesia's ambitious decentralization reform[33], which transferred administrative and budgetary responsibilities to lower levels of government, has yet to show a lasting impact on democratization in Indonesia.

Men are two times more likely than women to offer a definition of democracy, which confirms that, since the fall of President Suharto in 1998, little has changed regarding men and women political awareness and interest as men remain more involved and interested in political matters than women. Young Indonesians (i.e. between 17 and 29 years of age) are four times more likely to have democratic cognitive skills than respondents in other age groups.[34] This is indicative of the impact of political change on different generations as respondents in the 17 to 29 age bracket became political actors in the midst of Indonesia's democratic transition, which is likely to have influenced both their views and understanding of democracy.

Finally, factors generally associated with democratic cognitive skills, like education, exposure to media, non-electoral participation, affiliation with civil society organizations (CSOs), or attitudes toward elections do not emerge as relevant in shaping Indonesians' ability to define democracy. It could be the case that for the Indonesians that were sampled for the SAIS 2011 Survey these variables are just irrelevant, or these findings

---

32 World Development Indicators 2012 – Urbanization.
33 Bert Hofman and Kai A. Kaiser. 2002. The Making of the Big Bang and Its Aftermath: A Political Economy Perspective. Paper presented at Can Decentralization Help Rebuild Indonesia?, a conference sponsored by the International Studies Program, Andrew Young School of Policy Studies, Georgia State University, May 1–3, 2002, Atlanta, Georgia.
34 Question 8 of the SAIS 2011 Survey inquiries about respondents' age. Based on the responses received, respondents have been divided across five age brackets: 17–29; 30–39; 40–49; 50–59; and 60 and above. The first age bracket starts at 17 years of age because that is the voting age in Indonesia.

might reflect the immediate political past of Indonesia. During the Suharto authoritarian regime, many of these features were publicized as features of a democratic Indonesia, when instead elections, political and CSOs participation and a free media were mere window dressing.

In Korea, knowledge of the country's political governance structure,[35] individual consumption of consumer goods and education are the factors that influence citizens' democratic cognitive skills the most. Some 34 percent of Koreans correctly identify the president as the most important institution in their country thus suggesting that slightly more than one-third of Korea's population knows that Korea is a presidential democracy. The remaining 66 percent of Koreans seems to be less clear about their country's political institutional structure. In fact, 15 percent believe that the national assembly is the most important institution, followed by equal shares of Koreans (i.e. 11 percent) who think that either the judiciary or the political parties are the country's most important institutions, whereas another 6 percent gives primacy to local governments. Finally, 21 percent of polled Koreans declined to answer. These results are surprising, particularly because even if Korea's institutional reform process spans across three decades, no major institutional reform has been implemented since 2000. Yet, these results might be telling of the relatively shallow depth of Korea's democratic culture, possibly resulting from the lack of experience with democratic institutions prior to 1948. The elections for the first National Assembly and the drafting of the first constitution were based on the decision of the US Military Government in Korea to establish a separate Korean state south of the 38th parallel. This decision came after three years of US military occupation and in the face of a communist regime in the Russian-occupied zone, which had refused to have United Nations–supervised elections. Not surprisingly, the structure of Korea's first republic was strongly influenced by the American presidential system. The unicameral National Assembly was made up of 200 members; 85 of them were officially listed as independents, whereas the remaining 115 members represented fourteen different political parties. However, the abrupt establishment of a democratic government, without significant participation by the Koreans themselves, created a serious void on the representational side of the political process. In the late 1980s, Korea began its political transformation to move from military to democratic rule, where citizens would choose their president and other political leaders through competitive elections, civil liberties would be guaranteed and civic associations and interest groups gained access to the policy-making process. The last twenty years of Korea's political history tell without doubt that Koreans have embraced democracy as their legitimate system of government even if they seem not to be knowledgeable

---

35 Refer to footnote no. 12.

about their country political governance structure. This reality underscores existing concerns regarding the depth of Korean democratic culture and the strength of Korea's representative democracy.

In Korea, the actual democratic transition ended with the first democratic presidential elections in December 1987, and the government of President Roh Tae-woo was sworn into office in February 1988. President Roh Tae-woo was at that time candidate of the ruling authoritarian camp and, with a core member of the old regime in the top position of the new democratic regime, military forces were rapidly integrated into the democratic system. The moderate reform policies pursued by President Roh Tae-woo proved compatible with the self-interest of the old regime's supporters. The split political opposition's defeat forced them to reform their internal confrontational strategies, which resulted in the reorganization of the opposition parties and the significant moderation of the opposition's political proposals in the early 1990s. These changes helped create consensus among the country's conservative citizens that a return to an authoritarian regime was not an option for Korea's political future, and the changes had a stabilizing effect on the country's recently established democratic institutions and procedures. This showed in 1992, when Kim Young-sam a candidate of the governing party became the first civilian to assume the country's highest office after 30 years of military rule. His term of office (1993–1998) saw progress in major reforms in the areas of civil–military relations, intelligence agencies, laws governing elections and political parties, courts and the administrative systems. Finally, in February 1998, the inauguration of President Kim Dae-jung, a dissident for many years, demonstrated that all of Korea's major political forces had been successfully integrated into a democratic political system.

Discriminant analysis shows that Koreans who correctly identified the country's most important institution are a group only minimally distinct from those citizens who failed to do so, for in the extent to which factors like higher levels of education,[36] political knowledge[37] and

---

36 Question 19 of the SAIS 2011 Survey inquires about respondents' levels of education. Specifically, it asks: What is the highest educational level you have attained: R1. No formal education; R2. Incomplete primary education; R3. Complete primary school; R4. Incomplete secondary school: technical/vocational type; R5. Complete secondary school: technical/vocational type; R6. Incomplete secondary: university-preparatory type; R7. Complete secondary: university-preparatory type; R8. Some university-level education, without degree; R9. University level-with degree; R10. Post-university education; R11. Refused. The original answers to Question 19 have been re-coded in a three category education variable: 1. Primary education; 2. Some secondary education; and 3. university education.

37 The 2011 SAIS Survey includes three questions designed to test respondents' political knowledge. Question 67 inquires about the size of the population of Indonesia, Korea

24   *What does democracy mean to you?*

urbanity.[38] These findings casts further doubt on the real extent of the progress made in the democratization of authoritarian institutions and

---

and Thailand by asking: "Approximately how many people now live in (insert country name)?" Based on the responses received, a new variable, which identified the accuracy of respondents' knowledge of their population size, was computed. The new variable took the values of respondents' answers and subtracted them from the population value for Indonesia, Korea and Thailand as described in the World Bank 2010 World Development Report (WDR). The result of this computation showed that, regardless of the country considered, the accuracy of the responses had a very wide margin of error (i.e. between 10 and 40 percent). As a result of this finding, it was decided to code the responses as following: "accurate" for answers that were within 10 percent off the WDR 2010 figures; "nearly accurate" for answers that were within 11 to 20 percent off the WDR 2010 figures; "very inaccurate" for answers that were between 21 to 30 percent off the WDR 2010 figures; "grossly inaccurate" for answers that were more than 40 percent off the WDR 2010 figures. Question 75 for Korea inquired about past presidents by asking: In approximately which years was Kim Dae Jung President of the Republic of Korea? R1. Approximately between 1998 and 2003; R2. Others, specify; R3. Do not know/Cannot recall. The responses for Question 75 were dichotomized into "accurate", which identified respondents who correctly answered the question (i.e. 1998–2003), and "inaccurate", which identified respondents who answered incorrectly. Finally, Question 76 for Korea asked: Who is the Chairman of the Grand National Party in the Assembly? R1. Anh Sang Soo; R2. Other, specify; R3. Do not know/Cannot recall. The responses to Question 76 were dichotomized into "accurate", which identified respondents who correctly answered the question (i.e. Anh Sang Soo), and "inaccurate", which identified respondents who answered incorrectly. For each country, the responses to Questions 67, 75 and 76 have been computed in a scale with the items to be included subjected to factor and principal component analysis. In the case of Korea, the Kaiser-Meyer-Oklin value was .562, and the principal component analysis revealed the presence of one component with eigenvalues exceeding one, explaining 42 percent of the total variance. The Alpha reliability test shows an Alpha value of .591. Then, the point system originally devised to score the responses to Question 67 was applied to the responses to Questions 75 and 76. Correct responses were given four points to be consistent with the points assigned to the responses with the more accurate population estimates, whereas incorrect answers were given zero points. The points scored for each question were then summed, creating a new variable with values ranging from "0" to "12", where "0" indicates "no" political knowledge and "12" indicates the "highest" level political knowledge. The Korea Political Knowledge Scale has been dichotomized, and the two levels are: i) No, or low political knowledge, which identifies respondents who have not answered correctly any of the three political knowledge questions, or that have answered correctly at least one out of three questions; and ii) Medium to high political knowledge, which identifies respondents who have answered correctly two out of three questions, or all three questions. The possibility of trichotomizing or quartiling the political knowledge scale was considered to allow for as much variation as possible to be captured from the responses to questions 67, 75 and 76. However, the responses to the question regarding the population size of Korea allowed for partially correct responses to be counted. This was not the case for both Questions 75 and 76, which only allowed for either a correct or incorrect answers. Because of this, a trichotomized or quartiled political knowledge scale would have had a top or bottom heavy distribution and an extremely light distribution in the middle, which could have biased the results of cross-tabular and regression analyses.

38 Refer to footnote no. 25 for an explanation of the urban/rural variable in the SAIS 2011 Survey.

cultural values that used to support military dictatorships in Korea. Finally, these findings are consistent with those emerging from the 2010 Korea Democracy Barometer Survey,[39] which also concluded that Koreans are not informed about their country's institutions, and their interest and engagement in "democracy in practice" remains superficial and rather passive in nature.

As for the institution that most needs to be reformed, 16 percent of Koreans believe that it is the presidency, 12 percent believe that it is the political parties, and another 11 percent think that reform efforts should target the national assembly. Finally, 9 percent of respondents believe that the status quo should be maintained, whereas 34 percent of polled Koreans, the highest share across the three surveyed countries, declined to answer. Possibly, the reasons why around 8 million Koreans think that the presidency should be reformed relates to the fact that, since the transition in 1987, the executive branch has steadily expanded its powers while the legislative branch weakened, and the ineffectiveness of the judiciary increased. Korean presidentialism, in fact, has been characterized by frequent transgressions of the constitutional limits placed on governmental powers. The relationship between the president and the National Assembly generally oscillates between hyper-presidential dominance and institutional gridlock, both of which have a negative impact on democratic consolidation. Three times – from 1988 to 1990, in 1998, and again from April 2000 onward – the government faced an opposition majority in the National Assembly. In particular, President Roh Tae-woo (1988–1993) was confronted with a parliament dominated by three opposition parties, which were unable to act in a unified way against the government. This alignment paralyzed both government and parliament. Although the election victory of the opposition alliance led by President Kim Dae-jung in December 1997 led to a shift in power between the two major political blocks, the new president did not have the support of the parliament since the Grand National Party of Lee Hoi-Chang, who was the presidential election runner up, held a plurality of seats.

Such competing executive and legislative majorities often created institutional gridlock, with both sides forced to show a high degree of willingness to compromise and mutual trust, conditions which were often missing on both sides. As the first months of the new government showed, these preconditions could hardly be expected in a political environment where both the government and the political opposition were accustomed to "zero sum" political games. At the height of the 1997–1998 financial crisis, the gridlock between the president and the political opposition in the legislature led to a potential constitutional crisis, as the election of a new prime minister by the

[39] www.asianbarometer.org

National Assembly was on the agenda. Without any chance to get his favorite candidate elected, the president was forced to overcome the gridlock by doing what Guillermo O'Donnell called "governing on the edge of the constitution". As such competing majorities have been a chronic problem of presidentialism in Korea since democratization. The almost inevitable resultant political crisis has often been solved through the flexibility of the party system, albeit with severe political costs. The flexibility of party system offered the president the opportunity to construct a majority in parliament by allying his own party with one or more parties from the opposition and/or by co-opting independent representatives or opposition members of parliament into one of the governing parties. This political dynamic is telling of existing weaknesses in the horizontal integration of the various branches of government.[40]

Discriminant analysis shows that citizens who think the presidency is the institution that most needs to be reformed are part of that 34 percent of Koreans who are knowledgeable about the hierarchy of their country's institutional structure, and are also a distinct group from those who have different views on what parts of Korea's governance structure needs to be reformed because of their consumption of consumer goods and their and moderate levels of non-electoral participation (NEP).[41] Furthermore,

---

40 Aurel Croissant. 2002. "Strong Presidents, Weak Democracy? Presidents, Parliaments and Political Parties in South Korea". Korea Observer. Vol. 33, No. 1, pp. 1–45.
41 Question 90 of the SAIS 2011 Survey inquires about non-electoral participation and asked respondents the following: As you know there are other kinds of political activities beyond voting and party membership. I am going to read out some different forms of political action that people can take and I would like you to tell me, for each one, whether you have actually done any of these things, whether you might do it or would never do it under any circumstances. Please choose your answer from this card [SA]. R1. – Writing a letter to your newspaper or calling a radio or television show, or post a comment on the internet – Have done; Might do; Would never do; Do not know; No answer; R2. – Signing a petition – Have done; Might do; Would never do; Do not know; No answer; R3. – Attending a lawful demonstration – Have done; Might do; Would never do; Do not know; No answer; R4. – Participating in an election meeting or rally – Have done; Might do; Would never do; Do not know; No answer; R5. – Joining unofficial strikes – Have done; Might do; Would never do; Do not know; No answer.
   While the relationship between reported attitudes and overt behaviors remain debatable, the willingness to engage in political activities might indicate a level of political awareness that could be indicative of the level of political participation. The decision-making process of concluding whether a person will engage in a political activity represent a level of political sophistication as it requires individuals to weight the projected costs and benefits of each option against one another. Existing theories of electoral and non-electoral participation suggest that a person actually does think about this discriminately, otherwise they could easily avoid answering any such questions.

What does democracy mean to you? 27

regression modeling[42] shows that Koreans who think that the presidency or the national assembly are the institutions most in need of reform are respectively four and two times more likely to have democratic cognitive skills than Koreans who think that the institutional status quo should be maintained, or declined to answer. Regression modeling shows that knowledge of what parts of the country's governance structure need improvement influences citizens' democratic cognitive skills, while knowledge of the country

---

The original responses to Question 90 were used to construct a non-electoral participation index for each of the three countries. The NEP Index was first constructed taking the five measures of NEP (i.e. write a letter, sign a petition, join a protest, strike, vote) and recoding them to reflect a point system. Five points were given to a response indicating that a respondent "has done" any particular NEP activity, 3 points for a response indicating that he/she "might do" any particular NEP activity and 1 point to respondents who "would never do" any of the five activities. The difference in points assigned to the two last questions was done to take into consideration the difference between attitudes and actual behaviors. In cases where the respondent had one missing data out of the five questions, the missing data were replaced by an average of scores based on the responses to other activities. Respondents with two or more missing data for this set of questions were discarded as "system missing" as it would have not been reasonable to speculate on what action an individual would take in two or more activities based on known results for only one activity. The five resulting measures of NEP were first summed, with scores ranging from "5" (lowest) to "25" (highest). The frequency distribution of the participants in NEP activities was then trichotomized in the following way: "No NEP", which identifies respondents who scored 5 points across the five NEP activities; "Low NEP", which identifies respondents who scored between 7 and 9 points across the five NEP activities; "Mid to high NEP", which identifies respondents who scored between 11 and 25 across the five NEP activities. The difference among "no", "low" and "high" NEP scores lies in the number of activities each respondents has actually engaged in and the number of activities participants indicated as a possibility of future participation. The range of scores from "7" to "9" for "low" participants has the following characteristics: the minimum score of "7" means that a respondent has "4" "would never do" and "1" "might do". A respondent could receive a score of "9" through a couple of different alternatives, with the most passive possibility is that the respondent has not actually participated in any activity but has simply responded "might do" in three of the five activities. The range of scores from "11" to "25" for "medium-to-high" participants is characterized as follows: the minimum score of "11" means either that respondent entertains the possibility of engaging in three of the five activities, but "would never do" two of the five activities. Or, the respondent "has done" one of the five activities, "might" participate in one additional activity and "would never do" three of the activities. Finally, a score of "25" means that the respondent "has done" all five activities. The Korea NEP Index shows that 32 percent of respondents "do not participate" in any of the five measures of non-electoral participation; another 27 percent has a "low" level of NEP, whereas the remaining 41 percent of respondents have "medium-to-high" levels of NEP. These results indicate that 68 percent of Koreans would engage, or would be willing to engage, in NEP activities, thus suggesting that political engagement does not necessarily end on election-day for them.

42 Refer to Annex 2 for information about the regression modeling.

governance structure does not. These trends reinforce the fact that institutionalization of democracy seems to remain shallow, and that the interplay between institutions and political behavior might be weakening rather than strengthening democracy in Korea.

Respondents' changes in disposable income matter vis-à-vis their ability to define democracy. This is an important finding because Korea has long been regarded as one of the world's most successful economies,[43] and a nearly perfect test ground for the relationship between economic development and democratization. Despite the legacies of Japanese colonialism, the destruction that followed the Korean War and a lack of natural resources, Korea has been able to turn its once-backward economy into the world's twelfth largest in a relatively short period of time. The initial economic development of Korea took place under the leadership of authoritarian governments, particularly under the Chung-hee Park's and Doo-hwan Chun's regimes. Yet, there is consensus that the economic performance and achievements of the country's democratic governments fare well when compared with what the pre-1987 governments achieved. Particularly because of the country's political circumstances, many of the post-1987 economic results are judged better than the earlier ones and on a par with those of other OECD countries, mainly in terms of domestic investments, trade balance, management of inflation, gross domestic product and income growth rates. Yet, the years of democratic consolidation also saw widening socio-economic polarization with the country labor market becoming increasingly fragmented and stratified. Under-developed social protection programs and limited coverage have exacerbated economic disparities as reflected in many of the traditional economic indicators. The genesis of the growing dichotomy between global success and domestic fractures lies in the imbalance between economic liberalization and democratic politics. Following the 1997 Asian financial crisis, Korea implemented many market deregulation policies. Yet, the country democratic system was not capable of counterbalancing the rising dominance of business interests with the implementation of collective social policies. Political parties have been slow to act on distributional issues and to initiate social protection programs. The need for universal social protection emerged as a central issue in many of the political campaigns for local elections in 2010, and also in the legislative and presidential elections in 2012. Without a political intervention, growing inequalities are very likely to pose a serious threat to Korea's economic viability, social cohesion and, ultimately, to further democratic consolidation.

---

43 World Bank. 1993. The East Asian Miracle: Economic Growth and Public Policy. World Bank Policy Research Reports. Washington, DC.

Data from the SAIS 2011 Survey show that, between 2009 and 2011, consumption levels "stayed the same or increased" for 21 percent of Koreans, whereas 18 to 20 percent of respondents experienced a "severe decline" in consumption patterns, and 17 percent saw dramatic negative changes in their disposable income. Regression modeling shows that negative changes in disposable income impact citizens' democratic cognitive skills. In fact, as consumption levels decline so does citizens' ability to define democracy, with Koreans who suffered "severe declines" in disposable income being two times less likely to define democracy than those whose consumption of consumer goods "stayed the same or even increased" over the same period of time. This finding signals that democracy in Korea is not insulated from one's personal economic experiences and aspirations. Economic performance remains a fundamental factor for citizens' democratic cognitive skills thus re-iterating the relevance of successful economic performance vis-à-vis how Koreans see and understand democracy.

Finally, education plays a key role in influencing Koreans' democratic cognitive skills. OECD statistics show that, since the 1960s, Korea has attached great value to education because it was seen as a means toward economic progress and achieving individual and national success. In the 1960s, Korea had a national wealth level on par with Afghanistan: yet, the country's emphasis on education allowed its young people to leapfrog the academic achievements of the majority of other industrialized countries, including the United Kingdom, Norway and the United States. Among OECD countries, Korea is in first place in terms of the proportion of younger people who have completed an upper-secondary education. To attest Korea's achievements, citizens with a university-level education are two times more likely to define democracy than those with lower levels of education. This finding confirms the positive influence of education on democratization. Already in 1816, Thomas Jefferson wrote that "if a nation expects to be ignorant and free, in a state of civilization, it expects what never was and never will be"[44]. More recently, the relevance of the education–democratization nexus has been reinforced by the political paths followed by countries in the former Communist bloc, where countries with higher levels of education, like the Czech Republic and Poland, have managed an easier transition to democracy.

Korea is one of many democracies that have evolved out of a military regime, and this is possibly the reason why the concept of democracy enjoys significant popularity. Between 1987 and 1988, Korea accomplished a peaceful transition from military dictatorship headed by formal General Chun Doo Hwan to a democratic state that allowed Koreans to choose their

---

44 Thomas Jefferson to Charles Yancey, 1816. ME 14:384

president and other political leaders through free and competitive elections. Since 1988, Korea has implemented democratic institutional reforms that have expanded civil liberties and political rights and have established civilian control over the military. Yet, based on the findings from the SAIS 2011 Survey, there seem to be a mismatch between breadth and depth of Koreans' democratic cognitive skills, which might make it difficult for the most dynamic of Asian democracies to strengthen its democratic culture.

In Thailand, knowledge of the country's political governance structure, individual consumption of consumer goods and affiliation with CSOs are the factors that influence citizens' democratic cognitive skills. When it comes to identifying the country's most important institution, Thailand presented a challenge as 94 percent of Thais identified the monarchy as the most important institution, which is incorrect from an institutional perspective. Thailand became a constitutional monarchy in 1932, when a coup d'état ended the country's absolute monarchy. The monarchy, however, remained a relatively marginal institution until the 1970s, when the King started playing the role of political referee, regardless of whether the Constitution gave the King such power, or there was any need for the King to intervene into Thai politics. For instance, the King played a hand in forcing the army to yield power in 1973; then, in October 1976, the leftist rhetoric of the students alienated the King and the Bangkok middle class. Accusation of *lèse-majesté* gave pretext for action against the students and the abolishment of democracy without the King's objecting to it. In 1991, the King did not stop a coup d'état to remove Prime Minister Chatichai from power probably due to the corrupt nature of Chatichai's leadership and politics[45]. In 1997, during the national consultations for the preparation of the new constitution, the King let it be known that he supported former Prime Minister Anand's[46] constitution proposal. Prime Minister Chavalit[47] was left with no

---

45 Mr. Chatichai was Thailand's prime minister from 1988 to 1991 over the headiest years of Thailand's boom economy, when the annual growth rate soared as high as 13 percent. He also presided over what came to be known as the "buffet cabinet", a ministerial lineup whose excesses and corruption led to his government replacement by a military leadership in 1991.
46 In 1997, former Prime Minister Anand was elected to the Thai Constitution Drafting Assembly and appointed Chairman. In this capacity, he oversaw the drafting of the new constitution, which was completed within the prescribed time of 240 days, and approved, after intensive country-wide consultations and debate, by the National Assembly. The approved text of the new constitution was then submitted to His Majesty the King for His Royal assent and promulgated as the new Constitution of the Kingdom of Thailand on October 11, 1997.
47 General Chavalit Yongchaiyudh is a Thai politician and retired general, who was Thailand's 22nd prime minister from 1996 to 1997.

other option but also support Anand's proposal, even if it was designed to block the political modus operandi of the so-called up-country politicians"[48] In September 2006, the King is said to have backed the Privy Council[49] coup d'état against Prime Minister Thaksin, even if such a political move started a democratic rolling back which has yet to end. Finally, in December 2008, the King remained silent when the Constitutional Court dissolved the People's Party Power (PPP)[50], following the Bangkok courts' verdict of abuse of election for the PPP deputy chairman and two members of the ruling coalition, once again ousting a duly elected government.[51] The SAIS 2011 Survey (as well as other similar surveys), however, does not allow

---

48 "The 1997 Constitution was designed to promote the transparency and accountability of the political system and the stability and effectiveness of government. It strengthened executive authority, provided for a fully elected bicameral legislature, consolidated the electoral system in ways that favored a few larger parties, installed independent agencies to fight graft, guaranteed media freedom, required officials to disclose their assets and empowered the electorate to impeach unscrupulous cabinet ministers. When it was promulgated, the 1997 Constitution was opposed mainly by the old-style politicians who had peddled patronage and votes in return for power and graft. The vast majority of the Thai people, particularly Bangkok's middle class, civil society groups and business community, hailed it as the promised land of a full-fledged and lasting democratic system, a long-awaited document meant to eliminate graft from politics by promoting ability and integrity". In Thitinan Pongsudhirak. 2008. "Thailand Since the Coup". Journal of Democracy. Vol. 19, No. 4, pp. 140–153.

49 The Privy Council of Thailand is a body of appointed advisors to the Monarch of Thailand. The Constitution of Thailand stipulates that the Privy Council must be composed of no more than 18 members and led by the president of the Privy Council of Thailand, currently former Prime Minister and Army General Prem Tinsulanonda. The King alone appoints all members of the Privy Council. Under the 2007 Constitution of Thailand, the Privy Council is given many powers and responsibility, all with regard to the Monarchy of Thailand and the House of Chakri. In recent years, the Privy Council and its president in particular, has been accused of interfering in politics. These accusations stem from the council's general closeness to the Thai military, and particularly during the 2006 Thai coup d'état.

50 The People's Power Party was a Thai political party founded on November 9, 1998, by Police Lieutenant Colonel Garn Tienkaew. The party leader was Somchai Wongsawat, and the Party Secretary General was Surapong Suebwonglee. Most MPs of this political party originally hailed from the Thai Rak Thai Party and thus the party became its de facto reincarnation with former prime minister Thaksin Shinawatra as its leader. The PPP had a populist platform and was strong in the North, Central and Northeastern regions of Thailand. The PPP led the coalition government after the junta-government supported 2007 general election but in December 2008, the party came under fire as its deputy chairman, Yongyuth Tiyapairat, faced charges of electoral fraud concerning the 2007 general election. These charges led to the PPP dissolution by the verdict of the Constitutional Court in December 2008.

51 Thitinan Pongsudhirak. 2012. Thailand's Uneasy Passage, Journal of Democracy. Vol. 23, No. 2, pp. 47–61.

investigating further whether Thais' responses were motivated by respect for the King, who remains the most beloved public figure in Thailand, or by citizens' view that the monarchy is the most important institution in the country.

As for the institution that needs the most reform, 32 percent of Thais believe that is the political parties, 16 percent the prime ministership, whereas another 11 percent of Thais believe that the status quo should be maintained. Discriminant analysis shows that citizens who think the status quo should be maintained are a group distinct from all other respondents mostly because they are better educated, middle aged and urbanized. Twenty-two percent of respondents declined to answer, which is the second largest share of non-respondents after Korea. The latter findings could be symptomatic of "civic fatigue" brought about by recurrent coup d'états and the political instability that Thailand experienced over the last 10 years. The negative views on political parties might be the result of several attempted (and failed) reforms to establish an institutionalized political party system. In Thailand, political parties officially took form with the Constitution of 1946, which allowed their free organization. However, effective control over the state apparatuses, frequent coups d'etats, the forced dissolution of existing parties by the bureaucratic polity blocked the emergence of well-organized and politically powerful parties before mid-1970s. Since then, the formation of political parties was influenced by factors like vertical centralization of political power, access to state resources, horizontal decentralization of decision-making authority between state agencies and cabinet ministries and dispersion of political power within oversized multi-party cabinets. This has inevitably resulted in a party system that tends to gravitate toward big parties vulnerable to personality dominance, promotion of short-term interests, lack of significant ideological distinction or policy platforms, high fragmentation, strong factionalization and pronounced regionalization.[52] The fact that citizens are aware of the need for political parties to be reformed is an encouraging sign, as no workable form of democratic pluralism can operate without political parties. Yet, the current contentious political reality of Thailand does not suggest promising prospects for such reform to happen soon. Thais' view of the prime minister as an institution in need of reform might be reflective of citizens' sentiments that the leadership of the government is far more centered on the person of the prime minister than ever before, or of the fact that the single party from which that leadership is drawn overwhelmingly dominates the national legislature.

---

52 Aurel Croissant and Paul Chambers. 2010. Unraveling Intra-Party Democracy in Thailand. Asian Journal of Political Science. Vol. 18, No. 2, pp. 195–223.

Another factor could be the political struggles that have characterized the prime ministership of Thaksin Shinawatra, who successfully appealed to the rural electorate, and was elected prime minister by large majorities of Thais both in 2001 and in 2005. Yet, the Bangkok elites perceived Prime Minister Thaksin's electoral successes as proof of the failure, rather than success, of electoral democracy simply because his government might have threatened the dominant positions of the army, the civil service and the aristocracy. Finally, regression modeling shows that Thais who think that the prime minister and the political parties are the institutions most in need of reform are respectively four and three times more likely to have democratic cognitive skills than those citizens who think that the institutional status quo should be maintained or declined to answer.

Affiliation to CSOs[53] affects Thais' democratic cognitive skills in a negative way. Micro-level analysis of data from the SAIS 2011 Survey,

---

53 Questions 51 to 53 of the SAIS 2011 Survey inquire whether respondents belong to or associate with civil society organizations. Specifically, Question 51 asks respondents: Do you associate with, or belong to any of the following non-political, civic organizations? [SA] R1. Education, arts, music, sports, or cultural activities: Belong to/Associate with OR Does not belong to/Associate with; R2. Trade unions: Belong to/Associate with OR Does not belong to/Associate with; R3. Religious organizations (church, wat, mosque, temple): Belong to/Associate with OR Does not belong to/Associate with; R4. Professional associations: Belong to/Associate with OR Does not belong to/Associate with; R5. Humanitarian, charitable or social welfare services – Belong to/Associate with OR Does not belong to/Associate with; R6. Conservation, the environment: – Belong to/Associate with OR Does not belong to/Associate with.

Question 52 inquires about respondents' level of involvement in CSOs by asking: "Are you an active member of the following organizations? By active membership, I mean regular attendance of meetings and organization activities?" R1. Education, arts, music, sports, or cultural activities – Active member OR Inactive member; R2. Trade unions – Active member OR Inactive member; R3. Religious organizations (church, wat, mosque, temple) – Active member OR Inactive member; R4. Professional associations – Active member OR Inactive member; R5. Humanitarian, charitable or social welfare services – Active member OR Inactive member; R6. Conservation, the environment – Active member OR Inactive member.

Question 53 inquires about respondents' participation in CSOs, regardless of formal membership, and asked: Even if you are not a formal member, do you take part in any activities of the following types of organizations (SA) R1. Education, arts, music, sports, or cultural activities – Yes; No; No answer; R2. Trade unions – Yes; No; No answer; R3. Religious organizations (church, wat, mosque, temple) – Yes; No; No answer; R4. Professional associations – Yes; No; No answer; R5. Humanitarian, charitable or social welfare services – Yes; No; No answer; R6. Conservation, the environment – Yes; No; No answer.

To capture the full extent of respondents' involvement in CSOs, an Index for CSO Membership and Participation was constructed for each of the three countries surveyed using the individual responses to Questions 51, 52 and 53. For Thailand, the CSOs Index uses an order of value points system, based on the possibilities of respondents' answers. An

cross-checked with those from the Asia Barometers and the World Value Survey show low levels of affiliation to CSOs in Thailand. Specifically, 50 percent of Thai citizens do not affiliate/participate at all in CSOs, 28 percent are affiliated to just one CSO and 22 percent to two or more CSOs. Overall, this translates in 73 affiliations for every 100 people, which is similar to that of Indonesia (i.e. 77) and higher than the Filipino (i.e. 58) or the Korean (i.e. 37), and underscores the limits of any organization to influence the political discourse and give pause to all those who might attribute an automatic relationship between civil society membership and democracy. Furthermore, as shown in Table 2.1, involvement in religious organizations stands out compared to that of any other CSOs, which is testament to the long-standing Thai tradition of religious philanthropy but also a telling tale that organizational life beyond the temple remains extremely shallow.

Discriminant analysis shows that those who participate in CSOs are a group distinct from those who do not either affiliate with or participate in CSOs in that they are more likely to be traditional advisors, belong to the

---

"active member" would receive 3 points; an "inactive member" would receive 2 points; a "non-member participant" received 1 point, and an "uninvolved response" would receive 0 points. The value-based point system would measure respondents' level of membership and/or participation in each of the six categories listed above. To construct the value-based, point system measures, I started from the first series of six questions, which asked if the respondent was a member of a CSO in each category. If the respondents answered they were a member, a new variable was constructed, which identified members with a value of 2 points and non-members with 0 points. The next series of six questions were asked only to those respondents, who indicated they had a membership in the particular category of CSOs for which they had claimed membership. The question specifically asked if the respondent was an "active member" or not. If the respondents considered themselves "active members", they received a score of one point; they received zero points if they did not consider themselves "active members". The last series of six questions were asked only if the respondent indicated that they were not members of that category of CSOs, and it asks if the respondent participates in any activities of a CSO in that category. If the respondents indicated that they participate, they receive one point; if they did not participate, they received zero points. In the end, the scores computed for each individual CSOs category were summed together to create an index measuring activity of civil society in Thailand. The TH CSOs Index includes values, which range from 0 (i.e. no participation or membership in civil society) to 18 (i.e. active membership in all six categories of civil society), and it been trichotomized as follows: No Participation, which identifies respondents who are not members of, and do not participate in, any of the activities of the six, listed civic organizations; Low-to-Medium Participation, which identifies respondents who are either member and/or participate in the activities of one or two of the six, listed civic organizations; High Participation, which identifies respondents, who are either member and/or participate in the activities of more than two of the six, listed civic organizations.

Table 2.1 CSOs membership and participation in Thailand in 2011

Type of civil society organization	Non-participant	Non-member participant	Inactive member	Active member	Total
Education, arts, music, sports, or cultural activities	75.3%	4.1%	4.1%	16.1%	100%
Trade unions	96.3%	0.9%	0.6%	2.2%	100%
Religious	64.7%	8.9%	2.6%	23.8%	100%
Professional associations	93.1%	1.5%	1.4%	4%	100%
Charitable organizations	86.5%	5.2%	2.3%	6%	100%
Conservation, the environment, ecology	88%	2.4%	2.3%	7.3%	100%

Source: SAIS 2011 Survey – Thailand

upper and middle class, live in Bangkok and be well educated. Moreover, regression modeling confirms that as CSOs affiliation/participation levels increase, the ability of Thai citizens to define democracy decreases, with citizens with higher levels of CSOs affiliation/participation being less likely to have democratic cognitive skills, whereas those who do not participate in CSOs are more likely to be able to define democracy. Without organization, social capital remains irrelevant to democratic political culture, and these results tell that CSOs seem to be irrelevant to Thai citizens' democratic cognitive skills, which is bound to impact the quality of democracy in Thailand.

The third and last factor influencing Thais' democratic cognitive skills is economics. Data from the SAIS 2011 Survey show that between 2009 and 2011, consumption levels "stayed the same or increased" for 24 percent of Thais; an average 17 percent of citizens experienced a "severe decline" in consumption patterns, whereas 26 percent saw dramatic negative changes in their disposable income. This indicates that a relative majority of Thais suffered an overall decline in their disposable income. Regression modeling shows that negative changes in disposable income impact citizens' democratic cognitive skills. In fact, as consumption levels decline so do citizens' democratic cognitive skills, with Thais who suffered severe declines in disposable income being two times less likely to define democracy than those whose consumption "stayed the same, or increased" over the same period of time. This finding signals that democracy in Thailand, like in Korea, is not insulated from citizens' economic experiences and aspirations but rather negatively affected by them.

Thais have strong cognitive skills and yet they remain caught between a traditional elite-centric administrative state and their willingness of democratic mass participation. Thai people are at the heart of Thailand democratic consolidation, yet, it remains unclear whether their remarkable democratic cognitive skills might be enough to help Thailand emerge as a consolidated democracy.

How do the findings for the factors influencing citizens' democratic cognitive skills in Indonesia, Korea and Thailand compare with those of other countries in Asia and in other regions? Comparative research from the Barometer surveys and the World Value Survey suggests that the factors influencing citizens' democratic skills in Indonesia, Korea and Thailand are consistent with those shaping citizens' democratic conceptions in other countries around the world. Data from the Barometer surveys for the former Soviet Union and Eastern European countries regarding these countries' transition to democracy and the free market in the 1990s, show that, like in Indonesia, citizens were not likely to abandon their support for democracy because of how the country's economic performance affected their welfare. Similarly, data from the Africa Barometer for 1999 and 2001 for a large group of countries, including Botswana, Ghana, Nigeria, South Africa, Tanzania, Uganda and Zambia, show that economics considerations were missing from the list of substantively important factors influencing citizens' understanding of and support for democracy. Data from the Latinobarometro survey found that when many Latin American countries were hit by severe economic crises around the beginning of the 2000s, understanding of democracy went up but satisfaction with democratically chosen governments went down. Finally, in line with the findings for Korea and Thailand, data from the Asian Barometer survey found that citizens' evaluations of both their nation's and their household's economic condition emerge as one of the stronger predictors of support for democracy when the cross-national survey data are pooled together. The heterogeneous findings of existing comparative research suggest that economic factors should not be written off as key factors in citizens' democratic cognitive skills, and in turn in democratic consolidation.

Furthermore, the limited relevance of civil society membership and participation as well as civic literacy that emerged from the SAIS 2011 Survey data for Thailand is consistent with data from the Asia Barometer Surveys for 2005–2007 and the World Value Survey for 1995–2005. Research found that, starting in the late 1980s and early 1990s, civil society groups flourished across much of Asia in the wake of social modernization and political democratization. Yet, the levels of both membership and participation in civil society organizations fluctuate markedly with time, which suggests that high numbers of civil society groups did not necessarily translate in high level of individual participation in these very groups. In fact, data suggest that, in India, Malaysia, the Philippines, Singapore and Vietnam, only limited numbers of citizens belong to more than one association, thus revealing that Asian countries are "hardly nations of joiners" and that there seem to be no essential connection between the density of social networks and citizens' democratic cognitive skills.

Conclusions

This chapter shows that citizens in Indonesia, Korea and Thailand are cognitively capable of defining democracy and that only particular aspects of modernization theory are helpful to explain what shapes citizens' democratic cognitive skills across the three countries. In fact, citizens' conceptions of democracy appear to be based either on cultural values, socio-economic circumstances and, implicitly, upon what citizens learn from their experience about what democracy is and what it does at home. To different extents, these findings are consistent with Almond and Verba's[54] arguments that, at country-level, cross-national differences in individual attitudes toward democracy result from long-standing differences in norms and values, economic orientations that are transmitted through socialization across generations. At the individual level, this approach predicts that citizens' understanding of a particular political system (e.g. democracy) would be mostly shaped by personal norms and values.[55] Yet, the findings also underscore that the popularity of the concept of democracy and citizens' democratic cognitive skills are the first step toward building a democratic political culture, which remains a daunting challenge for most third-wave democracies such as Indonesia, Korea and Thailand.

A few words should be spent on those factors that did not emerge as relevant vis-à-vis citizens' understanding of democracy. Membership and participation in political parties, participation in the country's elections and non-electoral participation activities could serve as the basis for developing democratic cognitive skills.[56] Furthermore, a country's history of fair and competitive politics could help citizens develop awareness of democracy and strengthen their ability to draw lessons from the short-, medium- and

---

54 Gabriel Almond and Sidney Verba. 1963. The Civic Culture: Political Attitudes and Democracy in Five Nations. Princeton, NJ: Princeton University Press.
  Ronald Inglehart. 1988. "The Renaissance of Political Culture". American Political Science Review. Vol. 82, No. 4, pp. 1203–1230.
55 Alex Inkeles and David Smith. 1974. Becoming Modern. Cambridge, MA: Harvard University Press.
56 Steve Finkel, Christopher Sabatini and Gwendolyn Bevis. 2000. "Civic Education, Civic Society, and Political Mistrust in a Developing Democracy: The Case of the Dominic Republic". World Development. Vol. 28, No. 11, pp. 1851–1874.

long-term performance of elected governments and leaders. Finally, civic literacy also plays no role in political learning and judgment across the three countries. In general, increased news media usage and exposure should enhance citizens' democratic cognitive skills by expanding the range of considerations people bring to bear in making political judgments.[57] News and media tell people not only about the outcomes of political competition but also about the process by which these outcomes occur. Citizens gain awareness of procedures such as candidate nominations, the working of electoral systems, cabinet deliberations, parliamentary debates and judicial scrutiny. Media impacts could be greater in periods of rapid political and social changes, like political transitions, when people increase their dependence on formal news sources for information and certainty. Yet, none of this seems to be relevant when it comes to democratic cognitive skills of Indonesians, Koreans and Thais.

---

57 Diana Mutz. 1998. Impersonal Influence: How Perceptions of Mass Collectives Affect Political Attitudes. New York, NY: Cambridge University Press.

3 Is democracy a process or an outcome?

Chapter 3 tries to unpack the specific terms in which ordinary citizens understand democracy. To do so, it analyzes the content of citizens' responses to the open-ended question "What does democracy mean to you?" to capture what elements of democracy Indonesians, Koreans and Thais consider the most or least essential, whether they impute positive or negative meanings to democracy and understand it in procedural or substantive terms. The study of the cognitive orientations as related to political systems is not new, and differences in the understanding of democracy among citizens have been implicitly assumed by many scholars. Yet, as the operationalization and measurement of concepts as well as the availability of sufficient historical and comparative data to test the key linkages have proved largely elusive. The systematic analysis of the content of citizens' cognitive orientations and its relationship with affective and evaluative support for political systems has been limited. Easton argues that "there is little reason to believe that members of the system perceive the ideals, procedures and norms of the regime even in broadly similar terms".[1] However, since Converse developed the concept of "non-attitudes",[2] there has been much debate on the capacity of people to think about and participate in politics,[3] and the inability of citizens to have a clear understanding of what the political system and politics in general are about. Recent evidence from large opinion surveys is less pessimistic with regard to citizens' orientations to democracy. Not only

---

1 David Easton. 1965. A Systems Analysis of Political Life. New York, NY: John Wiley.
2 P. E. Converse. 1964. "The Nature of Belief Systems in Mass Publics". In David Apter (Ed.). Ideology and Discontent. Toronto: The Free Press of Glencoe.
3 George Rabinowitz and Michael B. MacKuen (Eds.). 2003. Electoral Democracy. Ann Arbor: The University of Michigan Press.
  Willem E. Saris and Paul M. Sniderman (Eds.). 2004. Studies in Public Opinion. Attitudes, Non-attitudes, Measurement Error, and Change. Princeton: Princeton University Press.

40 *Is democracy a process or an outcome?*

is there evidence that most people have some idea of what a democracy is, but also citizens seem to have different expectations depending on how they understand democracy.[4]

The first finding emerging from the SAIS 2011 Survey regarding the fundamental properties of democracy is that Indonesians, Koreans and Thais generally understand democracy in a positive way, with only small shares of citizens (i.e. plus or minus 5 percent across the three countries) offering negative definitions of democracy. Moreover, citizens see democracy as essential to both their country and their individual lives, with definitions from members of the upper and the upper-middle class more critical of democracy than those from members of the lower classes.[5] The second finding pertains to the estimates of citizens' overall capacity to understand democracy based on what properties of democracy they included in their answers. Data show that in Indonesia, Korea and Thailand, less than 20 percent of citizens' definitions of democracy include only one property of democracy, whereas close to 75 percent of them offer definitions of democracy including two or more properties of democracy – i.e. opportunity to change the government through elections; freedom to criticize those in power; reducing the gap between the rich and poor; guaranteeing basic necessities. This suggests that the majority of citizens across the three countries have a broad view of democracy. In fact, naming just one component represents a narrow, simplistic view of democracy, while identifying two or more represents a broad, more complex view of democracy.

In their breadth of understanding of democracy Indonesians, Koreans and Thais appear to be more different from one another than the aggregate ratio 75/20 might suggest. In Indonesia and Korea, citizens are more likely to have a multi-dimensional understanding of democracy. Specifically, 70 percent of Koreans mentioned two or three properties with one of them generally defining democracy in economic terms. Close to 80 percent of Indonesians also mentioned two or more attributes of democracy with

---

4 Michael Bratton and Robert Mattes. 2000. "Support for Democracy in Africa: Intrinsic or Instrumental". British Journal of Political Science. Vol. 31, No. 3, pp. 447–474.

   Richard I. Hofferbert and Hans-Dieter Klingemann. 2001. "Democracy and Its Discontents in Post-Wall Germany". International Political Science Review. Vol. 22. No. 4, pp. 363–378.

   Siddhartha Baviskar and Mary Fran T. Malone. 2004. "What Democracy Means to Citizens – And Why It Matters". European Review of Latin American and Caribbean Studies. Vol. 76, pp. 3–23.

5 Respondents' socio-economic classification was provided by an independent designation of income by A. C. Nielson, which implemented the SAIS 2000 and 2011 Survey in Indonesia, Korea and Thailand.

one generally being freedom. Thais, instead, are more likely to have a uni-dimensional understanding of democracy, with close to 65 percent of them only mentioning one feature of democracy, generally describing procedural aspects of democracy. These findings are only partially consistent with scholarly views arguing that in emerging democracies, uni-dimensional conceptions are more prevalent than multi-dimensional conceptions among the mass citizenry. Finally, data show that when the three countries are considered together, freedom is a recurrent attribute used to define democracy. However, when the data is disaggregated, freedom as a fundamental property of democracy does not necessarily appear in citizens' conception of democracy in one out of the three countries, which might suggest that non-liberal conception of democracy are as common as liberal ones across the three countries. These results are consistent with existing data from the 2005–2008 round of the Asian Barometer Survey, which shows that in the nine countries surveyed[6], exclusively liberal views of democracy represented less than one-quarter of the Asian mass publics. In seven of the nine countries, small minorities of less than one-third offered exclusively liberal conceptions of democracy, and in three countries the proportion of respondents who conceive of democracy in exclusively liberal terms was smaller than the proportion of respondents who conceive of it solely in terms of a political process. Finally, findings from 12 sub-Saharan countries[7] surveyed by the Afrobarometer between 1999 and 2000, show that 59 percent of citizens associate democracy with a single property, while 14 and five percent associated it with two and three properties respectively.

Citizens' conceptions of democracy in Indonesia, Korea and Thailand can be grouped into four main categories: (i) civil liberties; (ii) institutions and political process (e.g. voting, elections, political organizations etc.); (iii) rights (e.g. human rights, equality and peace); and (iv) economy and the private sector[8], which identify what properties of democracy Indonesians, Koreans and Thais see as the most essential. Table 3.1 offers a snapshot of citizens' choices across the three countries.

In Thailand, it is the category of institution and political process that emerges as the most relevant, thus suggesting that Thais see it as the one including the most essential properties for democracy, and the fundamental one to strengthen their country's democratic political culture.

6 Cambodia, China, Indonesia, Mongolia, Philippines Singapore, Taiwan, Thailand, Vietnam.
7 Botswana, Ghana, Lesotho, Malawi, Mali Namibia, Nigeria South Africa, Tanzania, Uganda, Zambia, Zimbabwe.
8 The categorization used to group responses to Question 81 of the SAIS 2011 Survey is consistent with those used in the Barometer Surveys and the WVS for their data manipulations.

Table 3.1 Citizens' understanding of democracy in Indonesia, Korea and Thailand

Country	Civil liberties	Institutions and political process	Rights	Economy and the private property
Indonesia	38%	32%	15%	1%
Korea	27%	19%	19%	15%
Thailand	27%	57%	5%	1%

Source: SAIS 2011 Survey

Thailand checkered history of democracy, its frequent coups d'état and forays into authoritarian-like regimes are likely to be among the reasons why institutions and political process are at the core of their understanding of democracy. Processes, and specifically democratic processes, are what Thais can refer to help their country complete a democratic transition that seems to remain so elusive. In Indonesia, civil liberties emerge as the most important category, followed closely by institutions and political processes. These results might be reflecting the fact that Indonesia is in the early stages of democratic consolidation when its citizens might keep several conceptions of democracy in the same regard. The same seems to be true also for Koreans even if Korea is in a further stage of democratic consolidation than Indonesia. The particular relevance of civil liberties is probably due repression and limited freedom that Koreans experienced under military rule and which attracted constant scrutiny and criticism from the international community over the years.

Somehow counter-intuitively for Asia's remarkable record of sustained economic growth over the last 40 years, only in Korea there is a significant share of citizens that see the "economy and the private sector" as a fundamental property of democracy. This finding suggests that Koreans seem to be more aware than Indonesians and Thais of the fact that economics played a key role in the political development of their countries. From 1965 to 1990, the 23 economies of East Asia grew faster than all other regions of the world. Most of this achievement is attributable to what has been labeled as "miraculous growth" in 8 economies: Japan, Korea, Singapore and Taiwan, China, Indonesia, Malaysia and Thailand. Since 1960, the economies of these eight countries have grown more than twice as fast as the rest of Asia, roughly three times as fast as Latin America and South Asia, and five times faster than Sub-Saharan Africa. They also significantly outperformed the industrial economies and the oil-rich Middle East and North Africa regions. Between 1960 and 1985, per capita income increased more than four times in Japan, Korea, Singapore and Taiwan, and more than doubled in

Indonesia, Malaysia and Thailand; because of rapid, shared growth, human welfare also improved. The Asian success is seen as the result of state-led economic development, typical of the late 20th century, characterized by the state intervening directly in the economy through a variety of means to promote the growth of new industries and create a stable, market-oriented environment, while maintaining a high degree of government intervention. In the case of Korea, the country's initial economic development took place under the leadership of authoritarian governments, particularly under the leadership of Presidents Chung-hee Park and Doo-hwan Chun. Alice Amsden[9] characterized Korea as a prototype case of a guided market economy in which the government has performed a strategic role in keeping in check domestic and international forces and harnessing them to national economic interests. Industries apart from the priority sectors experienced policy intervention only intermittently and were exposed unaided to the challenges of market competition. Industrial licensing policies allowed the state to limit the number of firms entering an industry, which facilitated the realization of economies of scale and encouraged competition for market shares among the existing firms in the industry. Finally, to stimulate growth the government set stringent performance criteria in exchange for subsidies. There is consensus, however, that the economic performance and achievements of the country's democratic governments fare well when compared with what the pre-1987 governments achieved. Particularly because of the country's political circumstances, many of the post-1987 economic results are judged better than the earlier ones and on a par with those of other OECD countries, mainly in terms of domestic investments, trade balance, management of inflation, gross domestic product and income growth rates. Because of its pre- and post-1988 economic accomplishments, Korea is generally regarded as a nearly perfect test ground for the relationship between democratization and economic development.

Discriminant analysis shows that Koreans who see the "economy and the private sector" as a fundamental property of democracy are a group distinguished from those who attribute other properties to democracy. They live in the capital city or in urban areas other than the capital city, have a positive view of the government[10] and of the professionalism of government

---

9 Alice H. Amsden. 1989. Asia's Next Giant: South Korea and Late Industrialization. New York, NY, and Oxford, UK: Oxford University Press.

10 Question 121 of the SAIS 2011 Survey inquires about citizens' views on the government's sincerity of efforts to improve the country. Specifically, Question 121 asks: How much to you agree with the statement: The government is making a sincere effort to improve the country. (SA) R1. Agree; R2. Neither agree nor disagree; R3. Disagree; R4. No answer.

officials,[11] vote[12] and think elections offer an opportunity to have a say in how the country is governed.[13] They, however, lack participation in CSOs.[14] The relevance that Korean citizens give to the economic aspects of democracy is consistent with citizens' views of democracy in Arab countries. Data from the Arab Democracy Barometer[15] for Algeria, Egypt, Jordan, Lebanon and Palestine for the 1999–2008 period show that close to one-quarter of respondents associate democracy with the satisfaction of economic needs and the most likely political system that can solve chronic economic problems such as unemployment and poverty.

Citizens' definitions of democracy could be further grouped along the lines of substance-based (i.e. civil liberties, rights and economy and the private property) or procedure-based (i.e. institutions and political process) conceptions of democracy. According to this categorization, citizens in Indonesia and Korea understand democracy as a political system where intended outcomes – civil liberties and rights – are more important than processes. This finding is consistent with scholarly arguments that people's attitude toward a political system is influenced by what that particular political system can deliver. Democracy is still believed to be the most effective

---

11 Question 123 of the SAIS 2011 Survey inquires about the professionalism of government officials. Specifically, it asks: Do you agree with the statement: Employees in government are professional and highly qualified? (SA) R1. Agree; R2. Neither agree nor disagree; R3. Disagree. R4. No answer.

12 Question 107, Question 108, Question 114 and Question 118 inquire about respondents' political behavior. Question 107 asks: When was the most recent local election? (SA) R1. Mayoral. Question 108 asks, Did you vote in the most recent local election? R1. Yes; R2. No; R3. No answer.

Question 114 asks: I want to underlie the complete confidentiality of your replies to all questions in the survey but this is particularly true of the next several questions. Your replies will never be connected to our name. Now, I would like to ask you some questions about yourself. For which party or candidate did you vote for the National Assembly Election in 2008? (SA) R1. I did not vote; R2. Grand National Party; R3. United Democratic Party; R4 Liberty Forward Party; R5. Democratic Labor Party; R6. Creative Korea Party; R7. Others, specify; R8. Not applicable; R9. Do not know; R10. No answer. Question 118 asks: For whom did you vote in the Korean Presidential Elections of December 2008? R1. I did not vote; R2. Lee Myung-bak; R3. Chung Dong-Young; R4. Lee hoi-Chang; R5. Others, specify; R6. Not applicable; R7. Do not know; R8. No answer.

13 Question 89 of the SAIS 2011 Survey inquires about citizens' attitudes about elections. Specifically, it asks: How do you feel about elections? (SA). R1. Waste of time; elections make no difference. R2. Elections are useful only for the elites of the country. R3. Elections offer an opportunity to show support for my local representative. R4.Elections allow me to show respect for an elder or patron or boss whom I respect; R5. Elections are important because I can have a saying in how my country is governed. R6. No answer.

14 Refer to footnote no. 53 in Chapter 2.

15 www.arabbarometer.org

political system in constraining possible abuses of political power and channeling political power toward the public interest. Moreover, analytical evidence show that, once citizens embrace a substantive understanding of democracy, they are unlikely to abandon it as long as their basic rights are protected against possible infringement, and even if confronted with short-term political turbulence or a down-turn in their country's socio-economic performance.[16] Nevertheless, it should also be noted that substance-based democratic conceptions do not necessarily mean the rejection of non democratic system embodied in well-established procedures and institutions. Different conceptions may simply reflect varying relative weights that people associate with the numerous cognitive components of democracy, or citizens' experiences with political regimes where democratic procedures like elections, or parliamentary discussions are used to perpetuate the existence of non-democratic political systems (e.g. elections in Indonesia under President Suharto), and which bereft these procedures of their true democratic meaning.

Thais, instead, see democracy for its process, thus suggesting that to them how democracy works might be more important than what it does. This finding could be the result of the fact that since Thailand became a constitutional monarchy, in 1932, it has seen a succession of coups d'état, military or civilian governments installed after the coups, and 18 different constitutions, the majority of which have brought only limited changes to the country's basic government structures. Over the years, the cyclicity of these events could have strengthened the value of process over that of substance for democracy in the eyes of the Thais. Furthermore, it has kept Thailand in a permanent state of democratic transition and prevented it from decisively moving toward democratic consolidation. Thais' understanding

---

16 Michael Bratton and Robert Mattes. 2000. "Support for Democracy in Africa: Intrinsic or Instrumental". British Journal of Political Science. Vol. 31, No. 3, pp. 447–474.

Canache Damarys. Forthcoming. "Citizens' Conceptualization of Democracy: Structural Complexity, Substantive Content, and Political Significance." Comparative Political Studies.

Ellen Carnaghan. 2011. "The Difficulty of Measuring Support for Democracy in a Changing Society: Evidence from Russia." Democratization. Vol. 18, No. 3, pp. 682–706.

Russel J. Dalton, Doh Chull Shin and Willy Jou. 2007. "Understanding Democracy: Data from Unlikely Places". Journal of Democracy. Vol. 18, No. 4, pp.142–156.

Arthur H. Miller, Vicki L. Hesli and William M. Reisinger. 1997. "Conceptions of Democracy Among Mass and Elite in Post-Soviet Societies." British Journal of Political Science. Vol. 27, No. 2, pp. 157–190.

Richard Rose, William Mishler and Christian W. Haerpfer. 1998. Democracy and its Alternatives: Understanding Post-communist Societies. Baltimore, MD: Johns Hopkins University Press.

of democracy in procedural terms is broadly consistent with Schumpeter's, Przeworski's and Collier's arguments that accept procedural conceptions of democracy as a measure of preference for democratic political systems, particularly in nascent and young democracies.

Looking at what are the factors that influence citizens' substantive or procedural understanding of democracy, it appears that they are largely country specific, and there is no factor-overlap across the three countries.[17] In Indonesia, discriminant analysis shows that citizens who understand democracy for its outcomes (i.e. 54 percent) are a group distinct from those who see democracy for its procedures; regression modeling identifies attitudes toward social capital formation[18] and political knowledge[19] as the predictors influencing their understanding of democracy. In the political realm, social capital intended as "an informal norm that promotes cooperation between two or more individuals", and it is expected to produce a "dense civil society which serves to balance the power of the state and to protect individuals from the state's power".[20] In Indonesia, however, citizens' who have social capital are 30 percent less likely to understand democracy for its outcomes when compared to citizens who do not have social capital. This finding

---

17 Refer to Annex 2 for the logistic regression models used to investigate what shapes respondents' substantive or procedural understanding of democracy in Indonesia, Korea and Thailand.
18 Question 50 of the SAIS 2011 Survey investigates respondents' attitudes regarding the formation of social capital by testing respondents' willingness to cooperate with neighbors on how to address a community issue. Specifically, Question 50 asks: I would like to tell you a story about a neighborhood in this city. A group of families have been living along the same street, which over the years has fallen in to such disrepair that it has become nearly unusable. Should each family [SA]: R1. Do nothing; R2. Wait for the government to make the repairs; R3. Personally, ask the government to make the repairs; R4. Repair the road but only in front of its own house; R5. Form a neighborhood association to pressure the government to make the repairs; R6. Band together with other families as a neighborhood to repair the entire street; R7. Don't know. The rationale behind Question 50 is that the willingness to form a group to put forth a collective demand requires a high degree of social trust toward his/her neighbors. In essence, this is the social capital required to lower transaction costs in collective action. The original responses to Question 50 have been re-coded so that answer options from R1 to R4 identify non-group responses, while answer options R5 and R6 identify group responses; the "do not know" answers were dropped. Question 50 is useful because it helps understand whether respondents who are aware of democracy also exhibit cooperative attitudes, or hold attitudes that would be characterized as having social capital. Responses to Question 50 show that, in Indonesia, most respondents, 58 percent, hold attitudes that would be characterized as having social capital, while 42 percent do not.
19 Refer to footnote no. 37 in Chapter 2.
20 Francis Fukuyama. 1999. "Social Capital and Civil Society," Prepared for delivery at the IMF Conference on Second Generation Reforms, October 1–5.

reinforces the view that in Asia citizens' attitudes toward social capital influences their understanding of democracy. Yet the impacts are not as strong as one might expect, particularly in light of the Western liberal democracies tradition where social capital played a fundamental role in democratization. Political knowledge has a positive influence on citizens' substantive view of democracy, and citizens' level of political knowledge increases as it does their likelihood of seeing democracy for its outcomes rather than for its processes. Data show that Indonesians with "medium to high" level of political knowledge are two times more likely to have a substantive view of democracy than those with lower levels of, or no political knowledge. This is not surprising as data from existing survey research suggest that Indonesians have generally showed a relatively good level of political knowledge of their country, and relevant literature indicates that civic literacy has a long tradition of positive influence on citizens' views on democracy.

Indonesians are "democratic neophytes" as the country only transitioned to democracy in 1998; however, they understand democracy in one of the most complex ways for its outcomes. Moreover, these results are also counter-intuitive to the arguments that direct democratic experience is one of the most relevant factors for the public to have a substantive understanding of democracy. Indonesia is a young democracy, and yet its citizens see democracy as citizens in countries which have been fully democratic for a longer time such as Eastern European countries, or even some Western liberal democracies.

In Korea, 61 percent of citizens understand democracy in substantive terms, and such views are mostly influenced by the extent to which citizens' participate in non-electoral activities (NEP).[21] Regardless of whether people write letters, sign petitions, or go to election meetings, participation beyond voting on election-day is instrumental to democratization. NEP is a system of checks and balances for citizens to hold political leaders accountable, and for political leaders to understand citizens' political mood and aspirations in between national elections. Data show that the majority of respondents in Korea "would never" take part in non-electoral participation activities, whereas, on average, 28 percent might participate, depending on the kind of NEP. However, only 4 percent of respondents, on average, would definitely engage in NEP activities. Moreover, regression analysis shows that those who do not engage in NEP (i.e. 32 percent) are 2.3 times more likely to have a substantive view of democracy than those Koreans that either have low or high levels of participation in non-electoral activities. These findings might be the results of the limited freedom to engage in any non-electoral

---

21 Refer to footnote no. 41 in Chapter 2.

participation activities that Koreans experienced under more than three decades of military rule. However, they are also consistent with the findings of comparative research from the Asian Barometer, which shows the relative relevance of NEP both in Korea and, more generally, across Asia.

These results show that Koreans appreciate the substance of democracy, which is what made Korean democracy strong enough to move beyond the threat of returning military regimes. Yet, the fact that just one factor is key in determining citizens' appreciation for the substantive aspects of democracy might signals a mismatch between breadth and depth of understanding of democracy, which is likely to make it difficult for the most vigorous of Asian democracies to make further progress in democratic consolidation.

In Thailand, 57 percent of Thais understand democracy in procedural terms, and such views are influenced by how citizens feel about elections[22] – the gold standard of all democratic procedures – and affiliation/membership with CSOs. Social scientists have long attached a high degree of significance to voting ranging from the act of casting the ballot to the voting turnout rates. News reports invariably cite voting statistics as a benchmark of democracy. Participation in elections is the most decisive means through which citizens take part in their country's political system. It is simple, direct and powerful, and it allows citizens to express differing opinions and visions for society through their choice of representative. Moreover, for a large majority of citizens in Asia, voting seems to be the only form of political participation they engage in.[23]

In Thailand, 52 percent of respondents see election as a genuine opportunity for democratic participation. A combined 54 percent of Thais, however, have more cynical views of elections: 37 percent think elections are simply "an opportunity for patronage", whereas 18 percent see elections as a "waste of time". In spite of such polarized views about elections, Thai people vote a lot (even for a country that has a compulsory voting system). As shown in Table 3.2, data from the International Institute

---

22 Question 89 of the SAIS 2011 Survey inquired about respondents' views about elections. Specifically, Question 89 asks, How do you feel about elections? (SA). R1. Waste of time, elections make no difference; R2. Elections are useful only for the elites of the country; R3. Elections offer an opportunity to show support for my local representative. R4. Elections allow me to support an elder or patron or boss whom I respect; R5. Elections are important because I can have a direct say in how the country is governed. Respondents' answers to Question 89 have been recoded as follows: R1. Waste of time (combines original responses to R1 and R2 options); R2. Opportunity for patronage (combines original responses to R3 and R4); and R3. Democratic Participation, which presents the original responses to R5.
23 R. H. Taylor (Ed.). 1996. The Politics of Elections Southeast Asia. Woodrow Wilson Center Series. New York, NY: Cambridge University Press.

Table 3.2 Vote turnout rates for parliamentary elections in Thailand (1946–2007)

Year	Voter turn-out	Total votes	Registration	Voting age population	VAP turn-out	Population	Invalid votes	Compulsory voting
2007	78.51%	35,844,272	45,658,170	47,021,213	76.23%	63,937,600	8.8%	Yes
2006	64.77%	29,088,209	44,909,562	56,461,491	62.61%	63,470,400	5.8%	Yes
2005	75.13%	33,693,624	44,846,472	45,866,519	73.46%	63,003,000	5.7%	Yes
2001	69.95%	29,909,271	42,759,001	42,663,353	70.11%	62,862,098	10%	Yes
1996	62.39%	24,060,744	38,654,836	36,997,720	65.03%	60,652,000	1.7%	Yes
1995	62.04%	24,060,744	37,817,983	36,997,720	64.07%	60,034,000	3.8%	Yes
1992	59.28%	19,224,201	32,432,097	32,923,200	58.39%	57,760,000	4.3%	Yes
1988	63.56%	16,944,931	26,658,637	30,965,820	54.72%	54,326,000	3.5%	Yes
1986	61.40%	15,104,400	24,600,000	27,830,830	54.27%	52,511,000		Yes
1983	50.75%	12,295,339	24,224,470	26,213,270	45.91%	49,549,000	4.10%	Yes
1976	43.69%	9,048,104	20,600,000	18,902,400	48.02%	42,960,000	8%	Yes
1975	47%	8,695,000	18,500,000	18,902,400	46%	41,896,000		Yes
1969	49.16%	7,285,831	14,820,180	15,097,300	48.26%	35,110,000	5.9%	Yes
1957	44.7%	4,370,789	9,919,417	11,108,080	39.35%	24,148,000		Yes
1952	38.95%	2,961,291	7,602,591	8,828,780	33.54%	19,193,000		Yes
1948	29.50%	2,117,464	7,176,891	8,191,680	25.85%	17,808,000		Yes
1946	32.52%	2,091,827	6,431,827	7,838,860	26.69%	17,041,000		Yes

Source: Author, based on data from the International Institute for Democracy and Electoral Assistance

for Democracy and Electoral Assistance for parliamentary elections in Thailand shows that, since 1946, voter turnout has steadily increased and more than doubled over the last six decades. Moreover, elections have proceeded with substantial regularity since November 1996 in spite of the 2006 coup d'état, protracted political turmoil and the increasing judicialization[24] of electoral politics, which seem to have become "Thailand's way out of any political crisis"[25] and carries profound and far-reaching implications as shown by the political events that followed the 2006 coup d'état.[26] Data show that 78 percent of respondents who think elections are a "waste of time" have a procedural understanding of democracy; this proportion drops to 72 percent for those who see elections as an "exercise of patronage" and to 63 percent for those Thais who see elections as "a genuine opportunity for democratic participation". Regression analysis shows that those Thais who see elections as a "genuine opportunity for democratic participation" are also 2.7 times more likely to see democracy for its procedures. These trends suggests that there is a stark share of Thais (i.e. 63 percent), who are saying procedures are important but these procedures are broken, or that, in spite of people voting in high numbers, participation in elections may be a ritual to authority rather than an opportunity for the individual to exercise his/her sovereignty to constrain government actions. Either way, these findings are not necessarily good news for both democratic consolidation and the strengthening of democratic culture in Thailand.

Affiliation to CSOs is another factor influencing Thais' procedural understanding of democracy. The results of the regression analysis, however, show that it is the citizens' who do not affiliate with CSOs – i.e. 50 percent of the total population – who are more likely (i.e. 1.8 times) to see democracy in procedural terms rather than citizens who affiliate to one or more CSOs (i.e. 1.2 times). This trend suggests that affiliation with/membership in CSOs only has the likely impacts predicted by the academic literature if a particular level of affiliation/participation exists.

---

24 Thitinan Pongsudhirak. 2012. Thailand's Uneasy Passage, Journal of Democracy Vol. 23, No. 2, pp. 47–61.
25 Ibid.
26 The Thailand Constitutional Court was disbanded and replaced by a smaller, nine-judge Constitutional Tribunal in 2006. This new agency found the political party Thai Rak Thai guilty of unconstitutional electoral procedures and dissolved it, and ordered a five-year ban on office-holding by any of its 111 executive-board members, including Prime Minister Thaksin and many other members of Parliament who had served in his cabinets.

Across Indonesia, Korea and Thailand, five factors – elections, political knowledge, participation NEP activities, affiliation with/membership in CSOs and attitudes toward social capital formation – provide a parsimonious explanation of what shapes citizens' understanding of democracy in substantive or procedural terms, which, in turn, seems to indicate that the political aspects of democracy might matter more than any other factor. These findings are consistent with comparative research from Africa, where data show that political information and participation influence citizens' views of democracy, but differ from empirical findings from Eastern European countries and the former Soviet Union, where data show that elections are relevant for both citizens with substantive and procedural view of democracy.

Conclusions

This chapter has showed that citizens in Indonesia and Korea see democracy as a political system where its intended outcomes – freedom, liberty and rights – are more important than how the democratic processes work. Opposite to this, Thais seem to think that electoral and constitutional procedures might be enough to guarantee democracy in Thailand. On the one hand, procedural understanding of democracy could be the result of the Thailand checkered history of democracy, which over the years, might have strengthened the value of process over that of substance for democracy in the eyes of the Thai citizens. On the other hand, the experience of Indonesians and Koreans with political regimes, where democratic procedures were used to perpetuate the existence of non-democratic regimes, might help explain their substance-based views of democracy.

The majority of polled citizens has a positive, multi-dimensional view of democracy. However, while freedom is generally seen as a fundamental property of democracy, it is not necessarily the most popular attributes of democracy in Indonesia, Korea and Thailand. Moreover, only Koreans equate democracy with socio-economic benefits and consider those benefits to be as essential to democracy as political and civil liberties. The elements of democracy that ordinary citizens in Indonesia, Korea and Thailand consider to be the most and least essential are bound to influence their preference and support for a particular regime type. Comparatively speaking, nascent and consolidating democracies have more space for institutional change to take place and for their citizens to experiment with different types of democratic institutional settings than in established democracies where the space for innovation could be limited. Hence, when citizens of new democracies perceive problems in governance, they are less likely to simply demand better enforcement of procedures and focus their demands on the outcomes they expect from the political system they have chosen for their countries. Yet, it could also be argued that in new or consolidating democracies there is more that can be done with procedures so that when citizens perceive problems in governance, they see the replacement of inefficient or flawed procedures as the best alternative because they understand democracy for its procedures.

4 Does democracy spread like a wave in Asia?

One question that continues to tantalize scholars of democracy is what causes democracy to spread across countries around the world.[1] A popular theme in democratic literature argues that one country's political and institutional choices could be influenced by forces originating outside a country's borders – rather than being a self-contained domestic process – and proposes various interpretations of how democratization occurs and of the role citizens play in this process. This idea is interesting but not new, as Emanuel Kant already in the 18th century suggested that the causes of democracy could be found beyond a country's borders. More recently, Rustow, Whitehead and Starr have referred to this theory to help explain the diffusion of democracy around the world.[2]

Patterns of diffusion can be discerned across many areas, from the spread of riots and coups,[3] to governmental types,[4] to political norms across countries,[5] to policies and institutions, with an emphasis on the role of power,

---

1 Daniel Brinks and Michael Coppedge. 2001. "Patterns of Diffusion in the Third Wave of Democracy". Paper presented at the annual meetings of the American Political Science Association, 2–5 September, Atlanta, Georgia.
2 Harvey Starr. 1991. "Democratic dominoes: Diffusion approaches to the spread of democracy in the international system". Journal of Conflict Resolution. Vol. 35, No. 2. Pp. 356–381.
3 Stuart Hill and Donald Rothchild. 1986. "The contagion of political conflict in Africa and the world". Journal of Conflict Resolution. Vol. 30, No. 4, pp. 716–735.
4 Daniel Brinks and Michael Coppedge. 2006. "Diffusion Is No Illusion: Neighbor Emulation in the Third Wave of Democracy". Comparative Political Studies. Vol. 39, No. 4, pp. 463–489.
5 Amitav Acharya. 2004. "How Ideas Spread: Whose Norms Matter? Norm Localization and Institutional Change in Asian Regionalism". International Organization. Vol. 58, No. 2, pp. 239–275.
  Martha Finnemore and Kathryn Sikkink. 1998. "International Norm Dynamics and Political Change". International Organization. Vol. 52, No. 4, pp. 887–917.
  Ann Florini. 1996. "The Evolution of International Norms". International Studies Quarterly. Vol. 40, No. 3, pp. 363–389.

coercion and incentive as causes of diffusion.[6] A few studies have specified the mechanisms through which authors believe diffusion occurs. The majority of the literature, however, seems to rely on implicit causal stories. Possible processes can be gathered from a long list of metaphors found in many of the existing studies[7] when trying to understand how states could act as laboratories of democracy.[8] If one country employs democracy-strengthening ideas, its neighbors may become more likely to adopt them as well. This may be true, but there are reasons to suspect that learning democracy may be more complicated than just discerning success as democratization processes are notoriously difficult to pin down due to the influences of country regional clustering, global trends and domestic factors. Finally, not everything works everywhere. While there is evidence that "failures" might diffuse despite their objective lack of success[9], it is also possible that earlier adoptions may prove to be unsuccessful, and countries will learn either not to adopt them or to adopt them in different forms.

Many scholars who have included aspects of diffusion in their theories have done so in relatively simple ways. Starr found that regime transitions take place closer together in time than chance would predict, and that countries whose contiguous or regional neighbors have experienced transitions in the three prior years are more likely to undergo a regime transition themselves.[10] Lipset controlled for Europe or Latin America; however, he did not specifically test to see whether there was a significant difference between regions. Coppedge and Brink[11] found some significant regional

---

6 Beth A. Simmons, Frank Dobbin and Geoffrey Garrett. 2006. "Introduction: The International Diffusion of Liberalism". International Organization. Vol. 60, No. 4, pp. 781–810. Also, Beth A. Simmons and Zachary Elkins. 2004. "The Globalization of Liberalization: Policy Diffusion in the International Political Economy". American Political Science Review. Vol. 98, No. 1, pp. 171–189.
7 The literature identifies some 104 terms that are generally used in reference to the theory of diffusion. Erin Graham, Charles R. Shipan and Craig Volden. 2013. "The Diffusion of Policy Diffusion Research in Political Science". British Journal of Political Science. Vol. 43, No. 3, pp. 673–701.
8 Frederick J. Boehmke and Richard Witmer. 2004. "Disentangling Diffusion: The Effects of Social Learning and Economic Competition on State Policy Innovation and Expansion". Political Research Quarterly. Vol. 57, No. 1, pp. 39–51.
9 Sarah A. Soule. 1999. "The Diffusion on an Unsuccessful Innovation". The Annals of the American Academy of Political and Social Science. Vol. 566, No. 1, pp. 120–131.
10 Harvey Starr. 1991. "Democratic Dominoes: Diffusion Approaches to the Spread of Democracy in the International System". Journal of Conflict Resolution. Vol. 35, No. 2, pp. 356–381.
11 Daniel Brinks and Michael Coppedge. 2006. "Diffusion Is No Illusion: Neighbor Emulation in the Third Wave of Democracy". Comparative Political Studies. Vol. 39, No. 4, pp. 463–489.

effects, particularly for Western, Middle Eastern and North African countries; they also argue that most apparent regional effects are spurious associations created by the fact that the countries in each region tend to cluster around certain levels of economic and political development. The way these scholars have operationalized democratic diffusion, however, makes it hard to distinguish between actual diffusion and regional clustering of domestic factors. A few studies introduced some more precise measures of democratic diffusion and controls for domestic variables. Przeworski et al. report that the more democratic neighbors a country has (and the more democratic countries there are in the world), the more likely an existing democracy is to survive, and that countries in certain geographical regions are either more democratic or less democratic than purely domestic models of democratization would predict.[12] Finally, O'Loughlin et al. tried to identify diffusion effects using a continuous measure of democracy over a long series of years.[13] Their work generated a contiguity matrix for the whole world and use measures of geographic clustering to explore the diffusion of democracy. However, the findings of their analysis were relatively modest as they were not able to state the exact nature of the diffusion process, despite finding a high degree of regularity and evenness across time and space. Their results probably best capture what is the state of the art in literature on the diffusion of democracy.

How democracy spread is an even more tantalizing question when it comes to Asian countries. In fact, since 1974, when the current wave of democratization begun, the movement toward democracy in Asia has remained limited, with only eight countries becoming electoral democratic in the past 30 years out of more than 60 countries that have become democratic around the world.[14] For many years, Korea vacillated between parliamentary and military governments until it completed its transition from military rule to democracy with the direct presidential elections of 1987. In 1986, People Power ended President Marcos' era and brought the Philippines back to electoral democracy after 14 years of martial law. Yet, since then, the Filipino democracy continued to encounter significant obstacles to consolidation caused by both a weak institutional structure and imperfect constitutional governance. In 1991, Mongolia made an overnight

---

12 Adam Przeworski, Michael Alvarez, Jose Antonio Cheibub and Fernando Limongi. 1996. "What Makes Democracies Endure?" Journal of Democracy. Vol. 7, No. 1, pp. 39–55.
13 John O'Loughlin, Michael D. Ward, Corey L. Lofdahl, Jordin S. Cohen, David S. Brown, David Reilly, Kristian S. Gleditsch and Michael Shin. 1998. "The Diffusion of Democracy, 1946–1994." Annals of the Association of American Geographers. Vol. 88, No. 4, pp. 545–574.
14 Freedom House. 2012 Freedom in the World Survey. www.Freedomhouse.org

transition to democracy following the collapse of the former Soviet Union. While there is agreement that Mongolia has done well out of necessity of becoming a democracy, the country's shortcomings in rule or law remain a significant obstacle to democratic consolidation. Indonesia successfully transitioned to democracy following the fall of President Suharto in 1998. Widespread corruption, incomplete institutional reforms and dysfunctional bureaucracy have been common features of the country's democratic consolidation. In 2002, with strong hopes Timor Leste became independent and joined the ranks of Asian democracies. Over the last decade, however, Timor Leste has seen mixed progress in overall governance and democratization. Large shares of population in Singapore and Malaysia have become vocal about possible shortcoming of democracy, while remaining supportive of the authoritarian regimes that currently govern their countries. Finally, even if Thais remain outspoken about the need for democracy to take firm roots in their country, Thailand's "stop-and-go" process toward finding a legitimate form of government remains without precedent in the annals of democracy.

Thus, in spite of promising beginnings, Asia remains among the world's regions that are not most democratic. According to Freedom House's Freedom in the World Survey, only 8 of the regions' 17 countries count as electoral democracy, with many Asian regimes not making a decisive move toward democracy and authoritarianism remaining a popular competitor to democracy. Countries in the region seem to be stuck in a democratization gray area with weak political institutions and limited citizens' political engagement, and thus they struggle with the demands of democratic consolidation and governance. Authoritarian regimes, however, seem to be coping easily with the challenges emerging from a more globalized regional outlook and the competition with democratization.

To gain some insights on the growth of democracy in Asia, this chapter discusses citizens' knowledge of Asian democratic and authoritarian regimes in Indonesia, Korea and Thailand, and presents the findings from both existing and new spatial econometric analyses, which using data from the Polity IV Project, investigates the spread of democracy across Asia and other regions around the world.

The idea that people in country "A" learn that country "B" has become a democracy and that this influences mass following of democracy in country "A" should presuppose that people in country "A" have an accurate or semi-accurate knowledge of country "B". After all and even if to different extents, the success of democratization remains a function of the receivers' perceptions of the relative benefits, compatibility and suitability of democracy to the realities of their own countries. Question 80 of the SAIS 2011 Survey asked respondents:

We all know about different things and you may or may not know about several countries in the next question. Which countries in Asia are democracies? [SA][15]

1. India
2. Indonesia
3. Myanmar
4. North Korea
5. People's Republic of China
6. Philippines
7. Singapore
8. South Korea
9. Thailand
10. Vietnam

Table 4.1 presents citizens' responses regarding knowledge of authoritarian regimes in Asia, and reveals a high degree of ignorance about what countries are or are not authoritarian. On average, only 43 percent of Indonesians understand that Myanmar, North Korea, Singapore and Vietnam are non-democratic political systems. In the case of China, 42 percent of Indonesians think China is a democracy while 39 percent think it is not. Finally, an average, 24 percent of respondents opted out of answering Question 80 and chose "do not know" as a response. In Thailand, on average, only 44 percent of citizens have answered Question 80 correctly, in addition to a third of the total respondents choosing "do not know" as their answer. Finally, with 61 percent of Koreans being correct about the nature of the political systems of China, Myanmar, North Korea, Singapore and Vietnam, the overall results for Korea are slightly better than both those of Indonesia and Thailand. However, Koreans seems to be better off with some countries than others. Eighty-eight percent of Koreans are correct in that China is not a democracy, whereas 40 percent of them believe that Vietnam is a democratic country. Koreans' better knowledge of authoritarian countries might be a reflection of the fact that one of last standing strongly authoritarian countries sits just North of Seoul, or that the years of military rule have sharpened the respondents' skills in recognizing the kind of political systems that they do not want for their country.

---

15 The countries listed in Question 80 represent a blend of Asian-only democratic and authoritarian regimes. Countries like Japan, Australia and New Zealand were not included in the final list as the pre-test of the SAIS 2011 Survey showed that high shares of respondents systematically chose the "do not know" answer option when asked about these three countries.

Table 4.1 Citizens' knowledge of Asian authoritarian regimes in Indonesia, Korea and Thailand

	China			Myanmar			North Korea			Singapore			Vietnam		
	Dem	Auth	DNK	Dem	Auth	DNK	Dem	Auth	DNK	Dem	Auth	DNK	Dem	Auth	DNK
Indonesia	42%	39%	19%	20%	51%	29%	28%	49%	22%	57%	25%	18%	25%	51%	24%
Korea	9%	88%	3%	21%	62%	18%	0%	97%	3%	85%	8%	7%	40%	48%	12%
Thailand	38%	37%	36%	8%	69%	22%	21%	49%	30%	47%	20%	30%	24%	46%	30%

Source: SAIS 2011 Survey

Furthermore, as shown in Table 4.2, citizens' knowledge of Asian democratic regimes, other than their own, seems to be shallower than that of authoritarian regimes. These results are surprising considering that the list of countries in Question 80 included India, the world largest democracy, Indonesia, the world's fourth largest democracy, and the Philippines, the oldest democracy in Southeast Asia. Data from the SAIS 2011 Survey show that 46 percent of respondents in Indonesia think that India is not a democracy, 39 percent that Korea is not a democracy, and 41 percent that the Philippines is not a democracy. Seventy-one percent of Koreans think that Thailand is a democracy, whereas just about 50 percent of Koreans correctly identify India and Indonesia as democratic regimes. In Thailand, on average, 31 percent of respondents think that India, Indonesia, the Philippines and Korea are not democracies, 15 percent that Thailand itself is not a democracy, and 29 percent chose the "do not know" answer option. On the one hand, this result might be directly related to the relevance of, and respect for, the monarchy rather than limited knowledge about the political system that Thailand had in place at the time of the SAIS 2011 Survey. On the other, this view could be a reflection of the democratic slump that Thailand experienced following the September 2006 military coup that pushed Thaksin out of active political life, and that more than before, the country needs to reconcile its citizens' will for democracy and the elites' views of how Thailand should be governed.[16] Discriminant analysis shows that in Thailand the citizens who answered "do not know" are a group distinct from those who answered Question 80 differently. They live in Bangkok, have some university level education and moderate exposure to the media, are modern opinion leaders and are minimally involved in non-electoral participation. These characteristics suggest that these respondents might have chosen to answer "do not know" to opt out of the question rather than because they ignore the nature of the political regimes of the Asian countries listed in Question 80.

What emerges from the analysis of the responses to Question 80 suggests that the vast majority of respondents across the three countries are sure that their own country is a democracy, and yet they seem rather unsure of whether countries in Asia are democratic or non-democratic, with knowledge of democratic political systems being poorer than that of authoritarian ones. This finding is consistent with early studies of political culture and political development, which discounted the ability of the public in nascent democracies to recognize democracy outside their countries. In addition, these findings, suggest that the transfer or the reception of the notion of democracy as a regime to govern countries is not necessarily successful across North and Southeast

---

[16] Thitinan Pongsudhirak. 2012. Thailand's Uneasy Passage. Journal of Democracy Vol. 23, No. 2.

Table 4.2 Citizens' knowledge of Asian democratic regimes in Indonesia, Korea and Thailand

	India			Indonesia			Philippines			Korea			Thailand		
	Dem	Auth	DNK	Dem	Auth	DNK	Dem	Auth	DNK	Dem	Auth	DNK	Dem	Auth	DNK
Indonesia	33%	46%	21%	88%	10%	2%	38%	41%	21%	40%	39%	22%	32%	46%	22%
Korea	51%	34%	15%	51%	31%	18%	71%	19%	10%	98%	2%	0%	71%	17%	12%
Thailand	27%	37%	36%	26%	38%	36%	42%	25%	33%	41%	25%	34%	82%	14%	4%

Source: SAIS 2011 Survey

Asia. These results cast doubts on the theory that democracy-friendly ideas arriving from democratic neighbors such in India and the Philippines played a role in Indonesia, Korea and Thailand becoming democratic.

Democratization can be viewed as the cumulative result of the ebb and flow of information at domestic, regional and global levels. These information flows are part of a web of interactions – such as cultural, language, social or historical circumstances – whose quality and cost can affect the extent to which democratization spreads across countries. The political and social characteristics of the countries at the receiving end determine whether institutional and normative changes are eventually implemented. As with other social phenomena, the potential receiver must choose between adopting or rejecting the innovation. With large-scale political change, the decision to adopt or not any changes is made at an institutional level (head of state or legislative body), with both elite's and mass' perceptions of the relative benefits, compatibility and suitability of democracy in the local context playing a key role. Thus, the decision to adopt or resist democratic change hinges on a combination of conditions in the receiving state, local perceptions of democracy as an alternative to the existing political system and the outcomes of the struggles by competing groups for their preferred political regime.[17]

Based on the original responses to Question 80, an index for citizens' knowledge of Asian authoritarian and democratic regimes was computed for each country.[18] The distribution of each country's index offers further

---

17 Lawrence Whitehead. 1996. "International Aspects of Democratization". In Guillermo O'Donnell, Philippe C. Schmitter and L. Whitehead (Eds.). Transitions to Democracy. Baltimore, MD: Johns Hopkins University Press.

   William McDougall. 1997. Promised Land, Crusader State: The American Encounter with the World since 1776. Boston, MA: Houghton Mifflin.

   J. A. Agnew. 1993. "The United States and American Hegemony". In Peter J. Taylor (Ed.). The Political Geography of the Twentieth-Century: A Global Analysis. London, UK: Belhaven Press.

18 This new variable did not include the original responses for Singapore and Thailand. The decision to exclude those responses was motivated by the ongoing debate (amongst the academic community) on whether Singapore and Thailand should be considered democratic political systems. Singapore holds elections that theoretically might alter "who governs". It has, however, remained a one-party state since its inception. The continued political instability and discarded elections results in Thailand made it debatable whether Thailand could be truly considered a democratic political system at the time of the SAIS 2011 Survey. For the remaining eight countries, a factor and principal component analyses were conducted to assess whether it was possible to construct a scale using all the eight countries. The Kaiser-Meyer-Olkin value was .712, and the principal component analysis revealed the presence of two components with eigenvalues values exceeding 1, explaining a combined 51 percent of the total variance. China, Myanmar, North Korea and Vietnam

Table 4.3 Knowledge index for Asian authoritarian and democratic political systems

	Low knowledge	Mixed knowledge	High knowledge
Indonesia	23%	52%	25%
Korea	35%	56%	8%
Thailand	27%	41%	32%

Source: SAIS 2011 Survey

insights on the ability of Indonesians, Koreans and Thais to associate authoritarian and democratic regimes with the right countries in Asia.

A quick glance at Table 4.3 shows that the majority and/or relative majority of respondents (i.e. 52 percent in Indonesia; 56 percent in Korea; and 41 percent in Thailand) have "mixed" knowledge of authoritarian and democratic political systems. In each country, the largest share of those with "mixed" knowledge have "high" knowledge of authoritarian countries and "low" knowledge of democratic ones, thus confirming the results that emerged from the analysis of the original responses to Question 80. The results for citizens with "mixed" knowledge have been used as the dependent variable in a regression model that investigates the factors that influence citizens' knowledge of authoritarian and democratic regime in Asia. These characteristics are important to the process of democratization, because in the long-run, they determine whether institutional and normative changes in the governance structures of these countries are accepted and, eventually, implemented. In Indonesia, respondents with "mixed" knowledge are

---

loaded on one factor whereas India, Indonesia, the Philippines and Korea load on another one. Therefore, it was decided to construct two separate scales: one for "knowledge of authoritarian political systems" and another one for "knowledge of democratic political systems". The two scales were ranked using a point system, which assigned "1" point to a correctly answered question and "0" points for any incorrect answer, or "do not know" answer so that each scale had possible scores ranging from "0" (i.e. no knowledge) to "4" (i.e. highest knowledge). In the next step, the two scales were dichotomized to show "high" or "low" levels of knowledge of democratic or authoritarian political systems. The two dichotomized scales were summed together to create a "knowledge index for Asian authoritarian and democratic regimes", which reflects three combinations of respondents' knowledge of authoritarian and democratic political systems in Asia. Specifically: "high knowledge" of both authoritarian and democratic political systems; "mixed knowledge" of authoritarian and/or democratic political systems; and "low knowledge" of both authoritarian and democratic political systems.

3 times more likely to be between 19 and 29 years of age, 2 times more likely to have completed secondary education, 4 times more likely to participate in a patron-client network as advisees[19] and 3 times more likely to live in Jakarta. Koreans are 3 times more likely to be from Seoul, 2 times more likely to have some university level education, 3 times more likely to participate in civil society organizations and 2.5 times more likely to be interested in politics. Thais with "mixed" knowledge are 4 times more likely to be from Bangkok, 2 times more likely to have some university level education, 3 times more likely to be engaged in non-electoral participation, 3 times more likely to be traditional leaders and 2.5 times more likely to be exposed to the media. Finally, the regression model revealed that, across the three countries respondents', democratic cognitive skills did not influence their knowledge of Asian democratic or authoritarian regimes. This is a counter-intuitive but interesting finding, and may be telling of both the limited ability of Indonesians, Koreans and Thais to recognize democratic political systems outside their own countries as well as how some of the features that characterize their definitions of democracy play out in practice. Overall, there may be an interest to catch up to the "democratic wave" among Jakarta, Seoul and Bangkok well-educated and politically knowledgeable elites and yet, at the mass levels, arguments about the democratic diffusion (even if only at citizens' general knowledge levels) do not seem to be supported by the findings emerging from the analysis of the responses to Question 80.

To explore aspects other than knowledge of authoritarian and democratic regimes as possible reasons behind democratic diffusion across Asia, the next section of this chapter presents Leeson and Dean's investigation of worldwide spatial dependence in democracy changes across geographic neighbors

---

19 Several questions in the SAIS 2011 Survey investigate traditional vertical networks. Question 23 asked respondents: "How often do other people come to ask your opinion about politics?" (SA) R1. Daily; R2. 4–5 times a week; R3. 2–3 times a week; R4. Once a week; R5. Once every 2 weeks; R6. Once a month; R7. Never; R8. Other frequency, specify.

Question 27 asked respondents: "Are there, here, people who come to you to ask for advice, help, or just to pay respect?" (SA) R1. Yes; R2. No; R3 No Answer.

Question 29, asked respondents: "Are there persons here to whom you go for advice, help, or just to pay respect?" (SA) R1. Yes; R2. No; R3. No Answer.

In addition to using the responses to these three questions by themselves, a variable for Opin_Advisor has been computed to signify if respondent is: i) Uninvolved; ii) Traditional leader; iii) Modern opinion leader; and iv) Traditional and modern opinion leader. The key difference between the traditional leader and the modern opinion leader is based on the kind of advice they give, with the modern opinion Leader giving advice on political matters more than other matters.

between 1950 and 2000,[20] and the results of new research extending to 2010 Leeson and Dean's original research. Leeson and Dean constructed panels of data from the Polity IV Project[21] for the period 1950–1990 and 1991–2000 and used spatial econometric methods to conduct the analysis.[22] Different data panels, including as much as possible the same countries, allowed for a more thorough analysis and to see whether the spread of democracy may have worked better during certain periods but not others. The combined use of a spatial autoregressive model (i.e. SAR)[23] and a spatial error model

---

20 Peter T. Leeson and Andrea M. Dean. 2009. The Democratic Domino Theory: An Empirical Investigation. American Journal of Political Science. Vol. 53, No. 3, pp. 533–551.
21 The data on democracy from the Polity IV project measures countries' levels of democracy annually, beginning with 1850. Generally speaking, democracy refers to systems that encourage inclusion, participation, open competition and institutionalized constraints. To measure the extent of democracy across countries, the Polity IV data consider the presence of political institutions and procedures through which citizens can express effective preferences about alternative policies and leaders and the existence of institutionalized constraints on the executive's exercise of power. The resulting democracy measure captures: a) political competition, or the extent to which structures and institutions of the state permit open competition for political power and protect the basic political rights afforded to the individual; b) participation, or the extent of meaningful inclusion of individuals and diverse groups within the political system; and c) the issue of liberties and the rule of law, or the extent to which certain political and civil rights of individuals are guaranteed within the political system. These measures are derived from a broader theory of authority relations initially developed to examine authority patterns of any social unit, including national political systems as discussed in Eckstein and Gurr's 1975 *Patterns of Authority: A Structural Basis for Political Inquiry*. The Polity IV Project dataset provides information for all the polities included in the dataset and has a low population low threshold (i.e. 5000,000 inhabitants) for the inclusion of a country in the international system. It employs a continuum of twenty-one possible scores for a given state ranging from "–10", or "total autocracy", to "+10", or "total democracy", to avoid the pitfall of having to impose arbitrary threshold values for democratic versus non-democratic status rather than simple dichotomous measures of democracy and autocracy. This allows to consider degrees of democracy and autocracy and to observe relatively small discrete regime changes. Third, the data are consistent with numerous other measures of regime type, political liberties and human rights practices in democratic system. Finally, the high inter-correlation among the Polity IV measures and other specific indicators of democratic character indicates that the patterns and trends identified by these panels of data are representative of democratic developments. Polity IV has constructed a variable to measure these factors specifically for the purpose of time-series analysis, which makes each country's democracy score comparable over time. This measure, called "Polity 2", is used in this analysis. Thanks to all these factors, the Polity IV Dataset allows for broad comparability across space and time.
22 Refer to Annex 2 for the spatial econometric models used in Leeson and Dean's research.
23 The spatial autoregressive model (SAR) explains how changes in democracy spill over onto geographic neighbors, and it is analogous to an autoregressive time-series model, but with lags over geographic distances rather than time. So, for a country "i", one spatial

(i.e. SEM)[24] allowed for the identification and estimation of democratic diffusion, and its effects and significance across different countries/regions. Leeson and Dean's analysis, however, did not try to identify which, if any, potential channels of democracy's geographic spread might have or have not been at work between 1950 and 2000.

The findings from the spatial econometric analysis show spatial dependence in changes in democracy worldwide for the period 1950–1990. Countries seem to catch between 10 and 12 percent of the average change in democracy in their geographic neighbors, whereas for the 1991–2000 period, the rates at which democracy spread decreased to about 9 percent a year.[25] Leeson and Dean argue that a relatively modest impact of

---

lag refers to all of "i's" contiguous geographic neighbors, two spatial lags refers to "i's" neighbors that are two countries away and so on. The SAR model specifies each country's dependent variable (i.e. changes in democracy) as a function of the weighted value of the changes in democracy in its neighbors. The SAR model allows potential democracy spillovers to flow multi-directionally. This is important since changes in democracy may flow in to and out of multiple countries, thus influencing democracy in each nation. The SAR model measures countries' changes in democracy over four-year periods to allow sufficient time for eventual changes in democracy to occur. It also measures countries' lagged levels of democracy over a five-year period. This is the level of democracy that prevailed in each country the year immediately preceding the four-year period over which countries' changes in democracy are calculated. Countries' lagged levels of democracy allow to control for as many factors as possible that might affect changes in democracy in its geographic neighbors, besides democratic contagion. This variable accounts for the fact that geographic neighbors often share a similar colonial and/or legal origin, form of government, degree of ethno-linguistic fractionalization and other such factors that tend to persist over time. It controls for any features of countries that contribute to their changes in democracy, which were present the year before the period of tabulated change. The lagged democracy variable is also useful because it helps determine whether there is democratic convergence across countries. If countries with lower levels of democracy in the previous period grow faster in terms of democracy the following period, the variable will suggest democratic convergence. If countries with lower levels of democracy in the previous period grow slower in terms of democracy the following period, the data will suggest democratic divergence.

24 The spatial error model (SEM) is analogous to the moving average time series model for contiguous geographic neighbors, which includes a spatially correlated error structure. The SEM model specifies each country's error for changes in democracy as a function of the weighted value of the changes-in-democracy error term of its geographic neighbors. It models how unexplained changes in democracy spill over onto geographic neighbors. The SEM model allows for multidirectional flows of influence rather than unidirectional flows. One key feature of the diffusion theory for the purposes of empirical investigation is that since this theory is geography-based, there is no need to worry about the potential for endogeneity bias. Geography is one of the strongest exogenous variables. Countries cannot choose their geographic location and cannot affect who they have as geographic neighbors. This removes reverse causality as a concern for spatial estimates.
25 Refer to Annex 2.

democratization at country and region levels might stem from the number of neighbors a country has. A higher number of neighbors dilutes the impacts of democratic change spreading from any one neighbor, and overall mutes the strength with which democracy might spread.[26] Furthermore, Leeson and Dean's analysis found that there is very little difference in spatial coefficients regarding the annual rates of democratic diffusion across different regions worldwide. This suggests that while different regions may each have their own equilibrium level of democracy, there may be some factors specific to each continent that account for the difference rates at which democracy spread. The relevance of these factors, however, seems to be extremely limited.[27]

Finally, the analysis also revealed democratic convergence, with more democratic countries becoming more democratic at a slower rate than less democratic countries. This suggests that, regardless of their geographic location, countries are moving closer to one another along the democratic dimensions. The application of Leeson and Dean's research methodologies and parameters to a new panel of data from the Polity IV Project for the period 2001–2010, confirms the existence of spatial dependence in changes in democracy between neighboring countries, with democracy spreading at a rate of about 9 percent, thus at slightly slower pace than what seen for both 1950–1990 and 1991–2000.[28] Moreover, the results also confirmed that democratic convergence continues and that the annual rates of democratic diffusion across different continents remain very similar to each other. Finally, running both spatial econometric models for the period 1950–1990, 1991–2000 and 2001–2010, when controlling for fixed effects (e.g. global business cycles, oil shocks, income growth rates) that are common across countries but vary across time, does not result in relevant changes in the

---

26 The regression model used first-order contiguity to determine the weight received by each country in the spatial weight matrix. However, not all of countries' geographic neighbors may be equal. In particular, those with more inhabitants, may be may be more influential than others on changes in democracy. For instance, a more populous country, such as the United States, might have more impact on Mexico's changes in democracy than one of Mexico's other contiguous neighbors, such as Belize, which is considerably smaller than the United States. To address this, contiguous neighbors in the spatial weight matrix are weighted according to population size. The results suggest that population size does not matter for the geographic spread of democracy. In fact, the results of the regressions produced nearly identical estimates as when simple first-order contiguity is used. The population-weighted regressions without fixed effects democracy's spread rate is between 8 and 9 percent; when the two-way fixed effect is introduced, democracy spread rate is between 7 and 8 percent.
27 Refer to Annex 2 for Leeson and Dean's analysis.
28 Refer to Annex 2.

estimates of the rates at which democracy spreads both worldwide and across regions. These findings suggest that even significant, but unpredicted events might not necessarily influence changes in democracy in any given country.

Conclusions

Across Indonesia, Korea and Thailand, the vast majority of citizens are sure that their own country is a democracy, yet, they seem rather unsure of whether countries in Asia are democratic or non-democratic, with knowledge of democratic political systems being poorer than that of authoritarian ones. Moreover, respondents' abilities to define democracy in their own words (i.e. their democratic cognitive skills) do not seem to influence people's knowledge of Asian democratic or authoritarian regimes. This is counter-intuitive and may be a telling sign of both the limited ability of Indonesians, Koreans and Thais to recognize democratic political systems outside their own countries and how the features that characterize their definitions of democracy play out in practice. Finally, the data show that democratic diffusion happens worldwide and across Asia. However, the annual rates of diffusion suggest that the strength with which democracy spread might have been generally overstated. In fact, an annual democracy spread rate varying between 11 and 9 percent is hardly one that describes democracy "spreading like a wave". The main empirical implication of these findings is that the geographic location of a country does not seem to be an important contextual dimension able to significantly influence the nature of political regimes across the world or Asia, or to constrain the political and institutional choices available to elites.

5 Is democracy the only game in town?

If the daily news is to be believed, it seems that most people around the world want democracy. This is obviously a generalization, but it is partially supported by many empirical studies and the findings from various opinion surveys. Yet, existing assessments on the levels of support for democracy have been criticized in recent years, as for democracy to take firm roots, it requires that large majorities of citizens consider democracy their preferred political regime, while rejecting non-democratic alternatives.[1] Referring to Winston Churchill's statement, "Democracy is the worst form of government except all those forms that have been tried from time to time"[2], scholars of democracy argue that many democracies survive not because a majority of people believes in its intrinsic strength but because there are simply no preferable alternatives. Citizens with little experience of, and limited sophistication concerning, democratic politics may be uncertain whether democracy or authoritarianism offers the best solution to the problems facing their countries[3] and often end up embracing both democracy and authoritarianism at the same time.[4] Richard Rose

---

1 Russell Dalton. 1999. "Political Support in Advanced Industrial Democracies". In Pippa Norris (Ed). Critical Citizens. New York, NY: Oxford University Press.
   William Mishler and Richard Rose. 1996. "Trajectories of Fear and Hope-Support for Democracy in Post-Communist Europe". Comparative Political Studies. Vol. 28, No. 4, pp. 553–581.
2 Churchill's dictum "Democracy is the worst form of government, except for all those other forms that have been tried from time to time" was originally made in a House of Commons speech, on November 11, 1947. The timing of this famous remark is significant. Churchill won World War II, but lost the July 1945 elections. When the news of his electoral defeat became public, Churchill remarked: "They have a perfect right to kick me out. That is democracy".
3 Robert A. Dahl. 1997. "Development and Democratic Culture". In Larry Diamond, Marc F. Plattner, Yun-han Chu, and Hung-mao Tien (Eds.), Consolidating the Third Wave Democracies. Baltimore, MD: Johns Hopkins University Press.
4 Michael Bratton, Robert Mattes and E. Gyimah-Boadi. 2005. Public Opinion, Democracy, and Market Reform in Africa. Cambridge, UK, New York, NY: Cambridge University Press.

points out that "institutions constitute nothing more than the hardware of democracy".[5] Many scholars, however, have argued that to function properly, a democratic political system requires a software congruent with the various components of the hardware. Citizens' affective support for democracy and rejection of authoritarianism are key components of the software required for democracy to work. Yet, affective support for democracy can be temporary or weak and lead to temporal instability for Gibson's aptly description of the democratic reality in post-Soviet republics and the former Soviet Union: "support for democracy could be a mile wide and an inch deep"[6], which suggests that it is not easy for "democracy to be the only game in town".[7]

For the past several decades, numerous national and international surveys have tried to address these questions in an effort to understand the possibilities and limitations of democratization in Asia and the processes by which Asian citizens embrace and legitimize democratic rule. These efforts have offered many insights on the inner workings of democracy in Asia. Yet, relatively little is known about why citizens of nascent and consolidating democracies remain attached to authoritarian rule after its demise, and of the different ways citizens orient themselves toward democracy and authoritarianism. Socialization and the performance theories help understand affective support for democracy. The socialization theory points to the importance of context in shaping democratic attitudes. Montero, Gunther and Torcal[8] argued that the more a person experiences democracy, the greater the probability that he/she will affectively support democracy as a political system. Rose, Mishler and Haerpfer offer a more

---

5 Richard Rose, William Mishler and Christian Haerpfer. 1998. Democracy and Its Alternatives. Baltimore, MD: Johns Hopkins University Press
6 James L. Gibson. 1996. "A Mile Wide But an Inch Deep(?): The Structure of Democratic Commitments in the Former USSR". American Journal of Political Science. Vol. 40, No. 2, pp. 396–420.
7 Larry Diamond. 1999. Developing Democracy: Toward Consolidation. Baltimore, MD: Johns Hopkins University Press.
　Juan J. Linz and Alfred Stepan. 1996. Problems of Democratic Transition and Consolidation: Southern Europe, South America, and Post-Communist Europe. Baltimore, MD: Johns Hopkins University Press.
　Doh Chull Shin. 2007. "Democratization: Perspectives from Global Citizenry". In Russel Dalton and Hans-Dieter Klingemann (Eds.), The Oxford Handbook of Political Behavior. New York, NY: Oxford University Press.
8 José Ramón Montero, Richard Gunther, and Mariano Torcal. 1997. "Democracy in Spain: Legitimacy, Discontent and Disaffection". Studies in Comparative International Development. Vol. 32, No. 3, pp. 124–160.

nuanced analysis of those views by introducing an evaluative dimension. They state that:

> support for the regime is initially shaped by early socialization and then evolves continuously throughout adult life as initial beliefs are reinforced or challenged by later experiences. In so far as recent results reinforce early socialization, political values will be relatively stable, but in so far as there are major changes or shocks in the performance of government, attitudes will change considerably.[9]

At the aggregate level, these factors all refer to characteristics of the context: the number of years a country has been a democracy; the predominant values in a country; and the quality of the democratic system. This is the context in which citizens develop their orientations to democracy in general, and to their countries' democratic system in particular. Socialization and cultural values may play a role in explaining why citizens of third wave democracies remain attached to the political values and practices of authoritarianism even after some years of democratic rule. The cumulative effect of socialization of non-democratic values[10] might make it difficult for citizens to re-orient themselves toward democratic values, especially toward the values of liberalism and pluralism that generally figure prominently in democratic regimes. The more strongly people adhere to values typical of the pre-democratic period, the more cautious they are likely to be about embracing democracy as the preferred form of government for their countries. Repeated, long-term involvement in the political process might help strengthen people affective support for, and integrate changes in, the political system in which they live. Moreover, familiarity with democratic processes might breed satisfaction with it. Positive experiences with the functioning of democratic institutions might also encourage citizens to endorse the view that democracy is better than its alternatives.

The performance of democracy also seems to be essential in how affective support for democracy develops and is understood in a country.[11]

---

9 Richard Rose, William Mishler and Christian Haerpfer. 1998. Democracy and Its Alternatives. Baltimore, MD: Johns Hopkins University Press.
10 Harry Eckstein. 1961. A Theory of Stable Democracy. Princeton, NJ: Princeton University Press.
11 Russell. J. Dalton. 1994. "Communists and Democrats: Democratic Attitudes in the Two Germanies". British Journal of Political Science. Vol. 24, No. 4, pp. 469–493.

Todd Kuniokaa and Gary M. Woller. 1999. "In (a) Democracy We Trust: Social and Economic Determinants of Support for Democratic Procedures in Central and Eastern Europe". Journal of Socio-Economics. Vol. 28, No. 5, pp. 577–596.

Geoffrey Evans and Stephen Whitefield. 1995. "The Politics and Economics of Democratic Commitment: Support for Democracy in Transition Societies". British Journal of Political Science. Vol. 25, No. 4, pp. 485–514.

Socio-economic development could strengthen democratic political orientations as economic development enables an increasing number of people to satisfy their basic needs and thus to acquire new knowledge and skills through formal education,[12] which in turn could expose them to the values of democracy. However, not everyone that experiences the benefits of socio-economic development embraces democratic political ideas and demands the democratization of authoritarian rule. Citizens could increase their support for democratic regime change in proportion to the benefits they see such change bringing to their prioritized interests. If they feel that democratization promotes their goals and aspirations, whether political or economic ones, citizens become more supportive of the process. If, however, they feel that it hinders their goals, they become less supportive. There exists, however, significant disagreement on the importance of economic and political factors in explaining citizens' support for democracy, with some scholars attributing exclusive significance to economic factors, while others only ascribing significance to political ones. In spite of these ongoing scholarly debates, Finkel, Humphries and Opp state that "the regime's performance on these dimensions [economic and political outcomes] is crucial in the development and solidification of support in emerging democracies".[13]

This chapter discusses what motivates ordinary citizens who have lived all or most of their lives under non-democratic rule, to embrace democracy as the preferred system of government by investigating citizens' affective support for democracy in Indonesia, Korea and Thailand – that is how Indonesians, Koreans and Thais feel about democracy as a political system to govern their countries. Indonesia was a fragile parliamentary democracy in the 1950s, before it was transformed into a dictatorship by President Soekarno and maintained as one by President Suharto before becoming an electoral democracy in 1999. Korea vacillated for decades between civilian and military rule until the army was finally forced out of politics in the late 1980s. Thailand's halting process toward finding a legitimate form of government is nearly without precedent in the history of democratization with 18 constitutions since 1932. Moreover, Chapter 5 looks into whether there is any relationship between citizens' democratic cognitive support and democratic affective support. Democratic support is, in fact, a multi-dimensional phenomenon. At one level, democracy represents a set of political values to which citizens aspire. At another level, democracy represents a political system and the processes by which a country is governed. Existing survey-based

---

12 Ronald Inglehart and Christian Welzel. 2005. Modernization, Cultural Change, and Democracy. New York, NY: Cambridge University Press.
13 Steven E. Finkel, Stan Humphries and Karl-Dieter Opp. 2001. "Socialist Values and the Development of Democratic Support in the Former East Germany". International Political Science Review. Vol. 22, No. 4, pp. 339–361.

research has revealed the existence of a significant gulf between these two dimensions of democratic support. Finally, findings from existing comparative research on affective democratic support, based on data from the World Value Survey and the Barometer Surveys, are weaved into the chapter narrative to discuss whether the findings for Indonesia, Korea and Thailand from the SAIS 2011 Survey are consistent with those of other countries in Asia or around the world.

Question 131 of the 2011 SAIS Survey inquired about citizens' preferences for authoritarian or democratic regimes by asking[14]:

I am going to describe various types of political systems and ask what you think about each as a way of governing this country. For each would you say it is very good, fairly good, fairly bad, or very bad way of governing this country?

> *R1. Having a strong leader who does not have to bother with parliament and elections*
> *R2. Having experts make all the decisions for the country*
> *R3. Having the army rule*
> *R4. Having a democratic political system*

As respondents are asked to answer each of the four parts sequentially, this question measures both whether the respondent wants to have a democratic political system in his/her country while also accounting for his or her rejection of autocratic systems of government in the country. In fact, as Klingemann,[15] Shin and Wells[16] have emphasized, democratic preferences could be meaningless unless they are paired with a rejection of authoritarian alternatives to democracy. In addition, Question 131 attempts to gauge different aspects of affective support for democracy using some items that include the word democracy in their formulation and others that do not. This is important because items containing the word democracy have been often criticized for increasing social desirability and, thus, reporting higher levels of affective support.[17] Moreover, critics have also questioned the use of

---

14 Question 13 of the SAIS 2011 Survey was borrowed from the World Value Survey to allow for comparison using available data from the World Value Survey.
15 Hans-Dieter Klingemann, 1999. "Mapping Political Support in the 1990s: A Global Analysis". In P. Norris (Ed.). 1999. Critical Citizens. Oxford, UK: Oxford University Press.
16 Doh Chull Shin and Jason Wells. 2005. "Is Democracy the Only Game in Town?" Journal of Democracy. Vol. 16, No. 2, pp. 88–101.
17 Brian Gilley. 2006. "The Determinants of State Legitimacy: Results for 72 Countries". International Political Science Review. Vol. 27, No. 1, pp. 47–71.

these indicators in democratic and non-democratic countries alike arguing that "idealist measures of political support do not discriminate well between established democracies and incomplete regimes".[18] Others have pointed out that affective support for democracy is especially hard to be operationalized with more than one indicator, because of its multidimensional nature,[19] and the difficulty of comparing existing measures of affective support for democracy across countries, independently of the quality of democracy or the way citizens understand democracy in each country.

The trends emerging from the responses to Question 131 suggest that citizens answer without doubt that having a democratic political system is "good" when asked directly or without the provision of other choices in the same question. In fact, 79 percent of Indonesian, 85 percent of Koreans and 79 percent of Thais did so. Yet, an in-depth look at the answers shows that, on average, 49 percent of Indonesians, 55 percent of Koreans and 55 percent of Thais have a preference for non-democratic regimes. They see "having a strong leader who does not have to bother with parliament and elections" and "having experts making all the decisions for the country" as equally "good" options for governing their countries. Moreover, 52 percent of Indonesians and Koreans and 43 percent of Thais see the option of having the army rule their country as a "good" for governing their countries.

These results suggests the lack of a strong, marked preference for a democratic political system like the one that emerges from the answers to the direct question regarding people's preference for a democratic political system and suggest that citizens might harbor concurrent appreciations for authoritarian and democratic political systems. This finding invites to speculate whether the concurrent appreciation of authoritarian and democratic political systems could be the result of respondents' relatively limited familiarity with "military rule" or "governments of technocrats". Indonesians, Koreans and Thais, however, are familiar with what having the army rule and with the concept of experts making all the decisions about the country. Data limitations – in the SAIS 2011 Survey as well as other similar surveys – preclude the possibility of investigating further answers to these two sub-questions which suggest a concurrent appreciation for both authoritarian and democratic forms of government, or why respondents seem to see the positive and negative aspects of those two options on

---

18 William Mishler and Richard Rose. 2001. "Political Support for Incomplete Democracies: Realist vs. Idealist Theories and Measures". International Political Science Review. Vol. 22, No. 4, pp 303–320.
19 Ryan E. Carlin and Matthew McMinn. 2011. "Support for Polyarchy in the Americas". Comparative Political Studies. Vol. 44, No. 11,pp. 1500–1526.

74 Is democracy the only game in town?

Table 5.1 Preferences for democracy and authoritarianism in Indonesia, Korea and Thailand

	Indoensia		Korea		Thailand	
	Good	Bad	Good	Bad	Good	Bad
Having a strong leader who does not have to bother with parliament and elections	42%	54%	58%	32%	62%	30%
Having experts make all the decisions for the country	54%	40%	54%	40%	55%	48%
Having the army rule	55%	42%	52%	41%	43%	42%
Having a democratic political system	79%	17%	85%	12%	79%	15%

Source: SAIS 2011 Survey

the same level. It could be speculated that, in the eyes of the respondents, military rule and technocratic government embody features such as political and economic decisiveness, or technocratic competence in political and economic affairs that citizens believe their presidents or prime ministers should have to effectively govern their countries. Before Korea made its successful transition to democracy, it was a developmental authoritarian regime. This blend of military and technocratic rule delivered astonishing rates of economic development that transformed Korea from a very poor country into a middle class society in the span of two generations, while political rights and civil liberties remained sharply restricted. The impressing legacy of the developmental authoritarian regime and the challenges and new dynamics characteristic of the ongoing democratic consolidation could be at the heart of Koreans' views that both democratic and non-democratic political systems could be equally suitable options to govern their country.[20] Indonesians are familiar with what having the army rule the country means because President Suharto run Indonesia for 31 years, with the military having been given a rather prominent role in parliament and other aspects of country' political life. Moreover, Indonesians are also familiar with the concept of "experts making all the decisions about the country". In fact, in the 1980s, Indonesia and President Suharto benefitted from the policy advice of the "economic technocrats". These were foreign educated economists who

20 Larry Diamond and Gi-wook Shin (Eds.). 2014. New Challenges for Maturing Democracies in Korea and Taiwan. Stanford, CA: Stanford University Press.

under the leadership of Widiojo Nitisastro[21] displayed a talent for selecting policy changes that resulted in rising living standards, sustained rapid growth and low inflation.[22] In Thailand, military and technocratic rules are all too common. In fact, from the end of absolute monarchy and the introduction of parliamentary democracy in 1932 legal institutions have provided for the decentralization of power from the monarchy to the military and the urban elites but not necessarily to the people. Governments are generally set in power by factions of the military usually through a bloodless coup d'état, or more recently through votes of no confidence in Parliament. Once a new configuration of power is in place in Bangkok, elections are often held to legitimize the new government. The conflict between an emerging, mass-based democracy and elites firmly attached to less than democratic traditions embedded in a hierarchical society could be reason for concurrent appreciation of technocratic and military rule in Thailand. Regardless of the specific root causes, citizens' emerging ambivalence regarding democratic and authoritarian political systems are likely to have an impact on democratic consolidation in Indonesia, Korea and Thailand. Furthermore, the findings emerging from the SAIS 2011 Survey are consistent with the responses to a similar question asked in the World Value Survey for Thailand (2007), Indonesia (2006) and Korea (2005).[23] As shown in the table below, data for citizens' preference for a particular political regime points to the existence of residual appeal for authoritarianism at the individual level, which might suggest shallow foundation of democratic legitimacy in these three countries.

To estimate citizens' affective support for democracy and detachment from authoritarianisms, the original responses to Question 131 of the SAIS 2011 Survey have been combined in a 4-point scale. First, the four answer categories for Question 131 were assigned a numerical value ranging from

---

21 Widjojo Nitisastro was an Indonesian economist and one of Indonesia's most well-known and respected economic policymakers. He became a full professor of economics at the University of Indonesia in Jakarta at the age of 34 in 1962. After the fall of President Sukarno and the transition to the new government under President Suharto, he became the foremost member of the Berkeley Mafia group of economists, who were very influential in economic policy during the period of President Suharto's New Order government. Other members of the group, all senior Indonesian economists, included Professor Ali Wardhana, Professor Moh Sadli, Professor Emil Salim and Professor Subroto. Nitisastro held ministerial rank in successive Indonesian cabinets until 1983. He continued to be influential as one President Suharto's most trusted advisers throughout the 1980s and worked closely with the president until his resignation from office in 1998.
22 Azis J. Iwan. 1993. "Indonesia". In John Williamson (Ed.), The Political Economy of Policy Reform. Washington, DC: Institute for International Economics.
23 See www.worldvaluesurvey.org.

Table 5.2 World Value Survey preferences for democracy and authoritarianism in Indonesia, Korea and Thailand

	Indonesia 2006		Korea 2005		Thailand 2007	
	Good	Bad	Good	Bad	Good	Bad
Having a strong leader who does not have to bother with parliament or elections	24%	76%	48%	52%	71%	29%
Having the army rule	96%	4%	6%	94%	53%	46%
Having experts making all the decision for the country	48%	52%	53%	48%	63%	37%
Having a democratic political system	97%	3%	79%	21%	93%	7%

Source: World Value Survey Indonesia 2006, Korea 2005 and Thailand 2007

1 to 4. The sequence of the answer options R1 to R3 was kept in its original form, which allowed for the following numerical correspondence and recoding: Very Good = 1; Fairly Good = 2; Fairly Bad = 3; and Very Bad = 4. The sequence of the answer options for the R4 answer option was reversed to allow for respondents' preference for democratic political systems to appear on the same side of the attitudinal scale as rejection of authoritarianism: Very Good = 4; Fairly Good = 3; Fairly Bad = 2; and Very Bad = 1. For each country, the four recoded answers were subjected to factor and principal component analysis to test whether it was possible to construct individual countries' scales to capture as much variation as possible in respondents' authoritarian and democratic attitudes, and measured it along a virtual continuum.[24]

24 For Indonesia, the re-coded four response options were subjected to factor and principal component analyses. The correlation matrix revealed values ranging from .152 to .439, and the Kaiser-Meyer-Oklin value was of .650, and Bartlett's Test of Sphericity reached statistical significance, supporting the factorability of the correlation matrix. The principal component analysis revealed the presence of one component with eigenvalues exceeding one, explaining 46 percent of the variance. This finding was further supported by the results of the Alpha reliability test, which shows an Alpha value of .731, thus supporting the use of the items analyzed as items of a single scale.

For Korea, the correlation matrix revealed values ranging from .051 to .303, and a value of 0.589 for the Kaiser-Meyer-Oklin; in addition, the Bartlett's Test of Sphericity reached statistical significance, supporting the factorability of the correlation matrix. The principal component analysis revealed the presence of one component with eigenvalues exceeding 1, explaining the 40 percent of the variance. This finding was further supported by the results of the Alpha reliability test, which shows an Alpha value of .469.

The scale includes values ranging from "0" (i.e. strongest authoritarian attitudes) to "16" (i.e. strongest democratic attitudes), and it has been quartiled to capture as much variation as possible in the respondents' attitudes.[25] The cutoff points for the four levels of the countries' specific scales were set as follows: "low", which identifies respondents with strong affective support for authoritarian regimes (i.e. preference for having a strong leader who does not have to bother with parliament or elections; or having the army rule; or having experts making all the decision for the country); "low to medium", which identifies respondents with borderline authoritarian affective support (i.e. preference for having a strong leader who does not have to bother with parliament or elections; or having the army rule); "medium to high" for respondents with borderline democratic affective support (i.e. preference for having experts making all the decision for the country; or having a democratic political system); and "high", for respondents with strong affective democratic support (i.e. preference for having a democratic political system and rejection for non-democratic political systems).[26] A series of cross-tabulations and discriminant analysis was performed to identify the appropriate cutoff points to quartile the scale and ensure that each quartiled group was distinctly different from the other.

Figure 5.1 offers a snapshot of the distribution of citizens' affective support for democratic or authoritarian political systems across the three countries. In Indonesia, there are two strong authoritarian citizens for

---

For Thailand, the correlation matrix revealed values ranging from .186 to .691; the Kaiser-Meyer-Oklin value was of .689, and Bartlett's Test of Sphericity reached statistical significance, supporting the factorability of the correlation matrix. The principal component analysis revealed the presence of one component with eigenvalues exceeding one, explaining the 57 percent of the variance; this finding was further supported by the results of the Alpha reliability test, which shows an Alpha value of .734, Thus supporting the use of the four items analyzed as items of a single scale.

25 Refer to Annex 2.
26 Cross-tabulations using socio-economic variables (e.g. age, gender, education, urbanity, consumption and income levels, etc.) and political variables (e.g. CSOs, NEP, political parties' affiliation, attitudes toward elections, voting etc.) revealed distinguishing factors between: i) respondents who scored between 4 and 9 points and those who scored 10 points; ii) respondents who scored 10 points and those who scored between 11 and 12 points; iii) respondents who scored between 11 and 12 points and those who scored between 13 and 16 points. Discriminant analysis also confirmed the differences between these groups, which allowed to set the scale cut-off points at: i) 9 for respondents who ranked "low" on the scale and have strong authoritarian attitudes; ii) 10 for respondents who rank "low to medium" and have borderline authoritarian attitudes; iii) 11 and 12 for respondents who rank "medium to high" and have borderline democratic attitudes; and iv) 13 for respondents who rank "high" and have strong democratic attitudes. Please refer to Annex 2 for the raw scores of each country's scale.

78 Is democracy the only game in town?

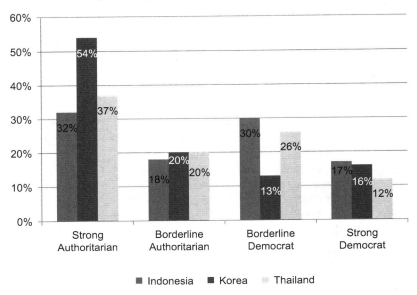

Figure 5.1 Democratic and authoritarian attitudes in Indonesia, Korea and Thailand

every strong democrat. Specifically, 32 percent of Indonesians have strong authoritarian attitudes, 18 percent have borderline authoritarian attitudes, 30 percent have borderline democratic attitudes, whereas 17 percent have strong democratic attitudes. In Thailand, there are three strong authoritarian respondents for every strong democrat. Specifically, 36 percent of Thais have strong authoritarian attitudes, 20 percent have borderline authoritarian attitudes, 26 percent have borderline democratic attitudes, whereas 12 percent have strong democratic attitudes. Moreover, both Indonesia and Thailand have over 45 percent of all citizens who appear to harbor concurrent appreciations of authoritarian and democratic political systems. These are likely to be citizens whose attitudes toward any particular type of political system remain undefined enough that could be strengthened in either direction of the spectrum of the political system. The relatively large share of concurrently appreciative citizens coupled with another third of respondents who have strong authoritarian attitudes could potentially become an obstacle to democratic consolidation either in Indonesia or Thailand, if the strong authoritarians gain enough momentum to leverage the authoritarian inclination of those citizens who could be swung in either direction of the political spectrum. In Korea, the ratio strong authoritarian/

strong democrat is 3.6 to 1, and thus larger than what seen in Indonesia or Thailand. The democracy scale shows that 54 percent of respondents have strong authoritarian attitudes, 20 percent have borderline authoritarian attitudes, 13 percent have borderline democratic attitudes and 15 percent have strong democratic attitudes. Furthermore, almost equal shares of Korean respondents show borderline authoritarian or democratic affective support and could be swung in either direction of the spectrum of the political system. Yet, the fact that 54 percent of respondents have strong affective authoritarian support reinforces, once again, the doubts that scholars and experts have expressed regarding how much progress Korea has made toward democratic consolidation.

Overall, the SAIS 2011 data show that in Indonesia, Korea and Thailand, authoritarianism has yet to lose its appeal, while democracy seems not to have yet lived up to citizens' expectations. At the regime level, it remains unclear whether citizens prefer democracy to non-democratic forms of government; this is in contrast with the strong support for democracy as an idea that Indonesians, Koreans and Thais have shown as discussed in Chapter 2 and 3. These findings tell that citizens' support for democracy at the concept level and support for non-democratic political systems at the regime level easily coexist at the mass level in each of the three countries. Furthermore, data from the 2011 SAIS Survey also show that the trend s for citizens' democratic or authoritarian affective support in Jakarta, Seoul or Bangkok mirror the trends seen at the national level as shown in Figure 5.2.

Figure 5.3 presents a comparison of the trends for democratic and authoritarian affective support at the capital level in 2000 and 2011, based on the data of the two rounds of the SAIS Survey. The SAIS 2000 and 2011 Surveys were not panel surveys; however, the results emerging from the analysis of respondents' general attitudes toward authoritarian and democratic political systems remain indicative of attitudinal changes vis-à-vis democracy or authoritarianism that might have taken place in any of these countries over a 10-year period.[27] In Bangkok and Seoul, respondents' authoritarian or democratic attitudes seem to have changed over a 10-year period, with democratic attitudes becoming weaker and authoritarian attitudes becoming stronger, particularly in Bangkok. This finding suggests that in 2011 in Bangkok, democracy at the mass level might be less vibrant than it was in 2000. This could be reflective of the general political turmoil that has taken place in Bangkok over the last 10 years. In Jakarta, attitudes appear to have remained stable overtime as any variations in Jakarta respondents'

---

27 Refer to Annex 1 for a description of the SAIS 2000 and 2011 Surveys.

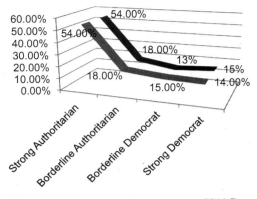

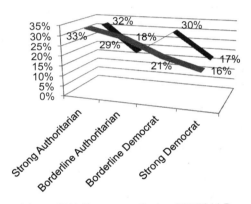

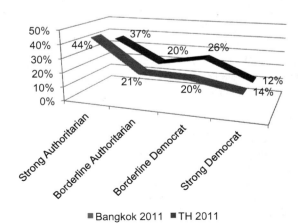

Figure 5.2 National and capital-level democratic and authoritarian affective support in Indonesia, Korea and Thailand (2011)

Is democracy the only game in town? 81

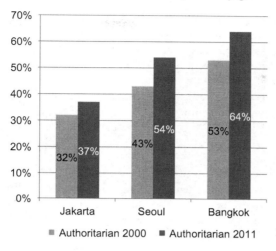

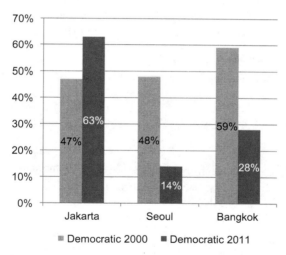

Figure 5.3 Democratic and authoritarian affective support in Seoul, Bangkok and Jakarta in 2000 and 2011

authoritarian or democratic attitudes are within the ±5 percent margin of error. Traditionally, Jakarta was the primary locale of the anti-President Suharto and pro-democracy movements. The results of the SAIS 2011 Survey suggest that, since the 1998 fall of President Suharto, the city's democratic affective support has remained strong and that the capital continues to be "a primate city in that it plays a vital role as the main disseminating center of social, political and economic innovations".[28]

How do the empirical findings regarding citizens' democratic and authoritarian attitudes in Indonesia, Korea and Thailand compare with those of other countries in Asia and around the world? Since the fall of the Berlin Wall in 1989, there has been a significant growth in public opinion research on popular support for democracy in new democracies. Among the best-known projects are the New Democracies Barometer, the New Europe Barometer, the Latinobarometer, the Afrobarometer and, more recently, the Asian Barometer Survey (ABS).

Findings from two rounds of the ABS for Indonesia, Malaysia, the Philippines, Singapore, Thailand and Vietnam based on desirability, suitability and preferability of democracy show that the level of citizens' preference for democracy as a regime greatly depends on the aspects of governance they are taking into consideration. When they view democracy as a political ideal, almost all of them embrace it as the best possible political system. However, when they are asked if they prefer democracy as the means to run their country, a large majority of them do not always or exclusively endorse it. Moreover, data also show that in five out of six countries, citizens favoring authoritarian regimes (i.e. military rule and single-party rule) constitute minorities. Full attachment to authoritarianism is least common in Singapore and Indonesia, and most common in the Philippines and Thailand. Citizens expressing no attachment to authoritarian regimes are a minority in the Philippines and Vietnam, whereas in the remaining four countries they constitute majorities ranging from 58 percent in Malaysia to 87 in Singapore. However, when democracy and authoritarianism are considered in a combined fashion, over three fifth of citizens across the six countries embrace democracy as the most preferred regime, even if the magnitude of these net preferences varies considerably across the countries.

In Africa, data from 12 African countries surveyed in 2000 by the Afrobarometer show that democracy enjoys a significant base of popular support. More than two out of three citizens (i.e. 70 percent) say that they prefer democracy to other forms of government. A majority expresses support in 11 out of 12 Afrobarometer countries, with Botswana, Tanzanians

---

28 In The Southeast Asian City, A Social Geography of the Primate Cities of Southeast Asia, T. G. McGee investigates the main features of the growth, characteristics and roles of the great cities in Southeast Asia, in an attempt to illustrate the function of the primate cities as the locale, where the colonial common heritage, cultural diversity and widely varying economic and political systems come together to push forward the overall development of Southeast Asian countries. T. G. McGee. 1967. The Southeast Asian City. A Social Geography of the Primate Cities of Southeast Asia. New York, NY: Praeger Publications.

and Nigerians being most supportive (i.e. above 80 percent) thus suggesting that a solid, pro-democracy base exists in Africa. Data also show that as many or more people reject various forms of non-democratic rule than prefer democracy. Eight out of ten Africans reject military rule and presidential one-man rule. However, like in the case of the responses in the SAIS 2011 Survey, these preferences for democratic political systems might not be indicative of a consistent opposition to authoritarian alternatives. Many Africans pick and choose among varying types of authoritarian rule and are willing to live with some but not others, and when the proportions that reject all alternatives to democracy are recalculated, just 58 percent of the Afrobarometer respondents reject all three forms. Thus, many of those who agree that democracy is preferable to any other form of government seem to be also willing to tolerate one or more forms of non-democratic rule. Finally, a minority of 48 percent of respondents across the 12 African countries emerges as having strong democratic attitudes and as those who reject all governing alternatives that are not fully democratic.

Evidence from panel surveys and large scale surveys conducted in the former Soviet Union between 1990 and 1992 found that attitudes toward democratic institutions and processes were reasonably stable and that democracy was more than just beliefs and values of ordinary citizens. Specifically, data show that the mass public of the former Soviet Union held unusually favorable attitudes toward democratic institutions and processes at the beginning of the democratic transition in 1990. These findings were surprising in the sense that they were inconsistent with the view that totalitarian socialization under the Soviet regime had been effective at reinforcing authoritarian values in the mass public. At the level of aggregate percentages, there was little evidence of a systematic erosion of support for democratic institutions and processes. There were no large shifts in opinion, and generally the percentages of respondents expressing support for democratic institutions and processes were similar in 1990 and 1992. Furthermore, data also show that attitudes toward democratic institutions were reasonably stable over time, with those favoring democracy in 1990 tending strongly to favor democracy in 1992, and when confronted with a crucial opportunity to act in defense of democracy (i.e. the August 1991 Putsch) many democrats did indeed mobilize. Yet, the effects of such mobilization were not particularly strong thus suggesting that democratic institutions and processes in Russian and Ukraine were "a mile wide but an inch deep".[29]

---

[29] James Gibson. 1996. "A Mile Wide But an Inch Deep (?): The Structure of Democratic Commitments in the Former USSR." American Journal of Political Science. Vol. 40, No. 2, pp. 396–420.

84 *Is democracy the only game in town?*

Table 5.3 shows that citizens' authoritarian and democratic affective support seems to be determined by country specific, unique combinations of factors and their factor overlap seems to be limited to citizens' perceptions of their countries' macro-economic outlook.[30]

Table 5.3 Factors influencing citizens' affective support for authoritarianism and democracy

	Indonesia	Korea	Thailand
Urban and rural status[31]			▨
Individual perception of macro-outlook[32]	▨	▨	
Individual consumption of consumers' goods[33]	▨		
Attitudes toward social capital formation[34]		▨	
Non-electoral participation[35]		▨	
Attitudes toward elections[36]			▨
Democratic cognitive skills[37]	▨		

Source: SAIS 2011 Survey

Chapter 2 and 3 showed the relevance of economic factors, specifically changes in disposable income vis-à-vis citizens' democratic cognitive skills and their understanding of democracy in substantive or procedural ways. It is, therefore, interesting that a different aspect of citizens' knowledge and attitudes toward the economy emerges as one of the determinant of citizens' democratic and authoritarian affective support across the three countries. The scholarly debate regarding the economics-democracy nexus is vibrant. Some scholars argue that democracy earn its legitimacy by "delivering the goods" – if people see a net improvement in their material welfare under democracy, they will support it. Others lean toward

---

30 Refer to Annex 2.
31 Refer to footnote no. 25 in Chapter 2.
32 Question 32 of the SAIS 2011 Survey is the first question of the survey Module 2, which inquires about respondents' knowledge and attitudes about the economy. Specifically, Question 32 asks: Generally speaking, do you think things are going in the right or wrong direction in (READ COUNTRY)? (SA) R1. Right direction; R2. Wrong direction; R3. No answer (DO NOT READ OUT); R4. Do not know (DO NOT READ OUT).
33 Refer to footnote no. 13 in Chapter 2.
34 Refer to footnote no. 18 in Chapter 3.
35 Refer to footnote no. 41 in Chapter 2.
36 Refer to footnote no. 22 in Chapter 3.
37 Refer to Chapter 2 and 3 for a discussion of democratic cognitive skills.

political explanations, caution against economic reductionism and claim that citizens' sense of commitment to democracy may be less a function of how they think the market is working than of how they experience democracy itself. Writing about how citizens respond to and form attitudes about democratic transition, Adam Przeworski similarly stressed that the most relevant factor is the gap between subjective expectations and real economic experiences. Consequently, if citizens believe that democracy improves their personal economic situation and that of the nation, then popular support for democracy increases. Russell Dalton found that citizens' attitudes toward democracy in former East Germany are strongly linked to their evaluations of the national economy.[38] Findings emphasizing the economic basis of popular support for democracy came under challenge from Geoffrey Evans and Stephen Whitefield[39], who analyzed survey data from eight post-communist countries in the early 1990s. Richard Rose, William Mishler and Christian Haerpfer[40] studied public opinion in nine former Eastern European countries and warned against reductionist theories "that treat all political attitudes as if they were simply derivative of economic conditions". They found that both economic and political factors determine levels of popular support for democracy, but politics matters more. Michael Bratton and Robert Mattes[41] found that Africans support democracy even while being discontented with its achievements in both the political and the economic realms, and that approval of democracy remains performance-driven, though approval hinges less on the delivery of economic goods than on the government's record of securing basic political rights. Perceptions of national economic conditions seem to influence citizens' democratic or authoritarian cognitive and affective support across Asia and the fact a great majority of Asian citizens have seen a significant socio-economic transformation unfold within their lifetimes, and that most of today's Asian democracies are the successors of growth-friendly, market-conforming, soft-authoritarian regimes could help explain this finding.

---

38 Russell. J. Dalton. 1994. "Communists and Democrats: Democratic Attitudes in the Two Germanies". British Journal of Political Science. Vol. 24, No. 4, pp. 469–493.
39 Geoffry A. Evans and S. Whitefield. 1995. "The Politics and Economics of Democratic Commitment: Support for Democracy in Transition Societies". British Journal of Political Science. Vol. 25, No. 4, pp. 485–514.
40 Richard Rose, William Mishler and Christian Haerpfer. 1998. Democracy and its Alternatives. Cambridge, MA: Polity Press.
41 Michael Bratton and Robert Mattes. 2000. "Support for Democracy in Africa: Intrinsic or Instrumental". Afrobarometer Working Papers No. 1.

Indonesia

In Indonesia, individual perceptions of the country macro-economic outlook have an impact on respondents' authoritarian affective support. In fact, respondents who are optimistic about how the Indonesian economy is doing are two times more likely to be strong authoritarians. However, citizens who experienced changes in their disposable income are, on average, 58 percent less likely to be strong authoritarians. These results suggest that, on the one hand, the perception of how the economy is doing influences respondents' authoritarian attitudes more than democratic ones. On the other, changes in respondents' disposable income – which represent a tangible effect of how the country's economy is doing – do not seem to impact Indonesians' democratic affective support. Indonesia's economic performance has been significantly less impressive in the democratic, post-Suharto's period than previously both in terms of annual rate of output growth and per capita income. The "Suharto's franchise"[42] was key in the success of the New Order in generating rapid and sustained economic growth over three decades as it ensured security of property rights and enforcement of contracts for favored businesses. The 1997–1998 Asian financial crisis was seen as a godsend to terminate a series of micro-economic policies whose main purpose was to enrich presidential cronies and the president's family. However, the informal institutions of the "Suharto's franchise", which were key to Indonesia's sustained economic growth also collapsed. In the aftermath of the 1997 crisis, the Indonesian economy kept muddling through with poverty reduction rates improving only slowly. Many scholars saw this as the result of institutional changes in the post- President Suharto's era focusing primarily on facilitating public participation in political processes with limited attention to reforms facilitating business activities, securing property rights and limiting discretionary behavior on the part of the civil servants so that the private sector can be efficient within a democratic environment. The findings of the SAIS 2011 Survey signal that the perception of poor economic performance resulting from the shortcomings of delayed economic reforms affects how Indonesians feel about democracy. However, their commitment to democracy seems to be insulated from their individual economic well-being.

---

42 Ross McLeod coined the phrase "Suharto's franchise" to describe the dynamics of security of property and enforceability of contracts during the Suharto's regime. McLeod argues that both security of property and enforceability of contracts existed not by way of a formal legal system but rather as a result of Suharto's relationship with his ministers, key bureaucrats and the military. Like franchises in the world of business, the unwritten rules of the "Suharto's franchise" were designed to provide strong, positive and negative incentives for its success.

Social capital is a key concept in the political realm as it could serve to balance the power of the state and to protect individuals from the state's power, foster cooperation between citizens' groups thus lowering transaction costs in both political and economic life. The stronger a society's or a country's social capital the greater the capacity to accomplish tasks jointly, regardless of where such tasks focus on fixing a road or managing democratic institutions. In Indonesia, social capital[43] has more of an impact on respondents' authoritarian affective support than on democratic affective support. Indonesians with strong attitudes toward social capital (i.e. strong willingness to cooperate) are 2.5 times more likely to have borderline authoritarian affective support and 2.2 times more likely to have strong authoritarian affective support. As Putnam and others have put forth, if social capital is substantial – quantitatively and qualitatively – democracy will be strengthened because citizen interests can be aggregated, their interests will be articulated and the collective action problems associated with putting forth their interests will be overcome. Such grassroots pressure would thereby lead to the government's addressing the demands and concerns of the citizens – horizontal accountability. The finding that social capital plays a marginal role in influencing citizens' democratic affective support is in contrast with this literature and could be one of the reasons for Indonesia slow progress on democratic consolidation and what is called "the low quality of Indonesian democracy".[44] Finally, respondents' democratic cognitive skills have a stronger impact on respondents' authoritarian affective support than on democratic affective support. This finding is counter-intuitive, especially in light of the findings presented in Chapters 2 and 3, which show that Indonesians have strong democratic cognitive skills and understand democracy for its outcomes. A comparative look at the data presented in Chapters 2, 3 and this chapter confirm that a gulf exists between understanding democracy as a concept or a set of values and as a political system in practice. This

---

43 Question 50 in the SAIS 2011 Survey investigates respondents' attitudes regarding the formation of social capital by testing respondents' willingness to cooperate with neighbors on how to address a community issue. It asks: "I would like to tell you a story about a neighborhood in this city. A group of families have been living along the same street, which over the years has fallen in to such disrepair that it has become nearly unusable. Should each family [SA]: R1. Do nothing; R2. Wait for the government to make the repairs; R3. Personally, ask the government to make the repairs; R4. Repair the road but only in front of its own house; R5. Form a neighborhood association to pressure the government to make the repairs; R6. Band together with other families as a neighborhood to repair the entire street; R7. Don't know.

44 Edward Aspinall. 2013. "The Irony of Success in Indonesia". In Larry Diamond, Marc F. Plattner and Yun-han Chu, Democracy in East Asia. A New Century. Baltimore, MD: Johns Hopkins University Press.

findings could, in turn, help understand the existing concurrent appreciation of authoritarianism and democracy that emerged from the original responses to Question 131 of the SAIS 2011 Survey and that have been discussed in the previous sections of this chapter as well as some of the political development happened in Indonesia since 1998.

In May 1998, the regime of President Suharto fell. Back then, the focus was on the fact that citizens played a fundamental role in the country's democratic transition, and thanks to this, Indonesia was bound to become a democratic country. While much of the democratic progress made since President Suharto's demise has generally been met with enthusiasm,[45] scholars have commented that in many respects the results of the transition to democracy have not lived up to the expectations as it is undisputed that there remain significant unfinished business regarding, for instance, the status and role of the council of regional representatives, the civil service and judicial system reforms, and also about the fact that the people's interest for these reforms to be completed might be weakening over time. The findings emerging from the SAIS 2011 Survey regarding citizens' authoritarian and democratic support are mixed at best and it remains unclear whether Indonesians will maintain their commitment to democracy as a political system suitable to govern Indonesia indefinitely, or whether the lack of relationships between citizens' economic well-being will stay the same over time.

Democratic transition is a complex endeavor, even more so in Indonesia. It is influenced by a specific combination of factors, which might not necessarily play out in the way democratic or modernization theory says they would. Indonesia is much freer and fairer than it was at any time since the mid-1950s. Basic rights such as the right to elect and remove a government, to associate freely, to have freedom of speech and belief and to have laws applied fairly are generally observed. It is clear that Indonesia is not going back where it was before the fall of President Suharto. Yet, the authoritarian affective support of a relatively large group of respondents should not be discounted or ignored particularly in light of the fact that the pace of political and institutional reform has been slowing down since 2004, and some scholars and commentators believed that it reached a virtual halt in 2011. Left to their own inclinations, the government and the political parties are likely to proceed with some sort of "democratic claw-back", seeking not necessarily to change the current system in a fundamental way but to curtail

---

45 Since 1998, Indonesia has resolved some of the primary institutional choices regarding the structure of government, most notably regarding the relationship between the executive branch and the legislature, the way elections are organized and the type of party system more likely to support democratic consolidation and the division of labor between national and sub-national levels of government.

scrutiny of their own activities and narrow the space for citizens' oversight and counter-pressure.

According to several scholars, these developments are the costs attached with the way that Indonesia dealt with some of the early challenges to democratization such as the military, Islamist political forces and regions breaking away following the example of East Timor. Aspinall[46] suggests that the trade-offs Indonesia accepted has not been an unfortunate side effect of the country's democratic transition; rather, it has been an important aspect of the successful transition as much as the nature of President Suharto's authoritarian regime and the path by which it was replaced. Not many clear lines were drawn between the pre- and post-1998 regimes and thus authoritarian forces have infiltrated the new democratic institutions and allowed to remain active. Democracy has still a long way to go in Indonesia and to survive the perils of its low quality it requires people's determination to remain the key stakeholders in their own democratic experiment.

Korea

Nowadays Korea is a democracy. Just in the late 1980s, this statement would have needed many qualifications with some scholars arguing that Korea had some of the most important attributes of a democratic system such as relatively free and fair elections and relatively free press. Others would have argued that these democratic practices were merely cosmetic, hiding the true power holders – that is, the military – behind a façade of civilian democratic rule. Possibly, both views were right and yet, fast-forward to the present day, and it is obvious for everyone to see that Korea meets the general standards of democracy based on free and fair elections, free press and people's participation. Korea has had five presidential elections that were largely free, competitive and fair. In 1997, a lifelong opposition candidate, Kim Dae Jung, won the presidency signaling Korea's attainment of democracy even by the strictest of procedural definitions of democracy. More than in many other countries, Korea's struggle for democracy has been the story of citizen participation, responsible elite decisions, but also danger and violence. So, it is not surprising that one of the two factors influencing respondents' democratic or authoritarian affective is participation in non-electoral activities. As shown in Chapter 3, one-third of Korean respondents do not associate themselves with any form of non-electoral participation, whereas a combined

---

46 Edward Aspinall. 2013. "The Irony of Success in Indonesia". In Larry Diamond, Marc F. Plattner and Yun-han Chu, Democracy in East Asia. A New Century. Baltimore, MD: Johns Hopkins University Press.

majority of 68 percent has either a "low-to-medium" (i.e. 27 percent) or a "high" (i.e. 41 percent) level of participation in non-electoral participation (NEP) activities. Furthermore, political participation by urban residents has also decreased as shown by the comparison of the data from the SAIS 2000 and 2011 surveys. In Seoul, the share of respondents with "no" NEP saw a 19 percent increase, going from 13 to 32 percent; those with a "low" level of NEP only increased minimally going from 24 to 27 percent, whereas the share of respondents with "high" levels of NEP saw a precipitous 22 percent decrease, from 64 to 42 percent. It is possible that the declines in NEP can be attributed to a general decline in social and political tensions, or that citizens' NEP is becoming more focused and issue specific, or to a benevolent government that is both knowledgeable and responsive to societal demands. If the former were the case, citizens' participation would have increased around local and national elections but did not. As for the latter, Korean governments led by both progressive and conservative presidents would have had high approval ratings. This is not the case as presidents leaving office have always left with generally low public approval ratings.

Data manipulation from the SAIS 2011 Survey shows that, among respondents with "no" NEP, 48 percent have strong affective authoritarian support. This proportion increases to 74 percent for those with "low-to-medium" levels of NEP; however, it declines to 57 percent for those respondents with "high" levels of NEP. Lack of NEP appears as the main trend among respondents with either borderline authoritarian or democratic affective support. Finally, the smallest share of respondents who do not engage in NEP is found among respondents with strong affective democratic support, which suggests that Koreans who see a democratic political system as suitable to govern Korea are generally involved in non-electoral participation activities.

Regression analysis strengthens the findings from the cross-tabulations and shows that Koreans with "no" NEP are 1.8 times more likely to have strong authoritarian affective support and 1.5 times more likely to have borderline authoritarian affective support, thus suggesting that, as democratic theory predicts, lack of NEP has more of an impact on citizens with authoritarian affective support. However, the impacts of "low to medium" levels of NEP and "high" levels of NEP on respondents with strong affective democratic support are similar to those that non-engagement in NEP has on respondents with strong or borderline authoritarian, affective support. Overall, these findings suggest that while NEP remains a relevant factor for Korea democratic consolidation, its influence on respondents' affective support, and particularly on democratic affective support, appears to be definitely limited.

What are the characteristics of Koreans who participate in non-electoral activities? Gender and age have no bearing on NEP. Shin has argued that men are generally more participatory in "each and every category of public activity" other than voting. While this may have been true in the 1990s, men do not appear to be any more politically active than women in 2011. Those who also access the news on a daily basis and Seoul residents are more likely to be politically active. With respect to education, those with some level of college education are more likely to be political participants, thus confirming that higher education does lead to a more action oriented, democratic citizen, and supporting Shin's statement that "the more educated are always more active than the less educated".[47] In 1995, only 20 percent of the adult population over the age of 25 had at least college and university education. In 2011, 39 percent of Korea's population between 25 and 64 are university graduates.[48] The fact that doubling the percentage of university graduates over a 15-year span did not increase the rates of non-electoral participation casts a doubt on the ability of education to enlarge political participation. The immediate political implication arising from this finding is that the concerns of the educated and the rich may be taken into account disproportionately with respect to the less educated and the underprivileged.[49] Democratic theory holds that equality is essential in the maintenance of democracy, and inequality can destabilize democratic institutions. Therefore, if the university educated plays a disproportionate role in non-electoral forms of political participation, this may result in an "elitist" rather than an "egalitarian" democracy. Finally, a frequent voter is not any more likely to have participated in the political activities than someone who is considered to be a non-habitual voter, and those who vote most frequently and those who participate in the non-electoral forms of political activity appear not to be from the same groups. This finding is not consistent with democratic theory, which suggests that voting and non-electoral forms of participation to be mutually reinforcing with those with high levels of NEP being found among the habitual voters, or with the arguments put forth by Wendy Rahn, John Brehm and Neil Carlson that elections can play an important role in fostering social trust and encouraging participation. Overall, low levels of NEP might impede the consolidation of democracy because it results in very little bottom-up pressure for institutional reforms. Thus, the SAIS 2011 data suggests that Korean politics is largely a realm of the elites as it seems that is the most educated who tend to be the most active.

---

47 Edward Aspinall. 2013, p. 114.
48 www.oecd-ilibrary.org/sites/factbook-2011-en/10/01/05/index.html?contentType=
    &itemId=/content/chapter/factbook-2011-85-en&containerItemId=/content/serial/18147
    364&accessItemIds=&mimeType=text/h
49 On average, college graduates earned almost twice as much as those with only junior high
    education and almost 60 percent more than high school graduates. Ibid., p. 270.

Koreans who are optimistic about the country's macro-economic outlook are 3.5 times more likely to have strong authoritarian affective support. Earlier chapters in this book have discussed the relevance of authoritarian-led economic development for Korea; so, it is not surprising that citizens' perception of the country's macro-economic outlook plays a role in respondents' authoritarian and democratic affective support. The fact that a positive view of the country's macro-economic outlook has a limited influence on respondents' democratic affective support suggest that Koreans' commitment to democracy is insulated from the country's economic performance. This is somehow surprising as there is consensus, among scholars and the international community, that the economic performance and achievements of Korea's democratic governments fare well when compared with what the pre-1987 governments achieved. Particularly because of the country's political circumstances, many of the post-1987 economic results are judged to be better than the earlier ones, or on a par with those of other Organisation for Economic Co-operation and Development countries in terms of investments, trade balance, management of inflation, gross domestic product and income growth rates. By the mid-to-late 1990s, Korea had become a high-income industrial society, and between 2000 and 2010, the country's average economic growth rate was around 4 percent, higher than other prominent market economies like Turkey or Mexico.[50]

Successful economic development was crucial for Korea transition to democracy; however, the findings emerging from the SAIS 2011 Survey shows that democratic consolidation is posing different challenges. During the transition to democracy, the focus was on the normative belief that democracy and its supporting market and institutional mechanisms were better than any other political and economic system and expanded opportunities for people's participation in the political process. During the consolidation phase, the practice of democratic politics extended to larger circles of citizens, and the number of civic organizations involved in aggregating political demands in a systematic fashion, rather than in the form of street protests, increased. Nevertheless, the quality of such expansion is a matter of opinion among scholars of democracy. It is clear that the country has moved well beyond the threat of returning to the military strongman politics of the 1960s and 1970s. The demand for civilian government elected through free and fair elections is firmly entrenched and there is general acceptance of the notion of opposition parties. People's desire for democracy remains strong but their commitment may not be deep. In fact, affective support with

---

50 International Monetary Fund. World Economic Outlook Report, 1998 to 2012. www.imf.org/external/pubs/ft/weo/2012/weodata/index.aspx

how democracy works fluctuates with events, including economic crises and political scandals, and trust with political institutions, particularly the presidency and the national legislature being generally low. These democratic "disjunctures" need to be addressed for democratic consolidation to progress further, and for Koreans not to become cynical about how the state of democracy in their country.

Thailand

There are few countries other than Thailand that could be a laboratory to study democratic consolidation. There has been a slow but continuous emergence of social, economic and political forces favoring democratic participation. However, these trends have also showed the many weaknesses of the Thai democracy and institutional setting. Thailand seems to remain caught between a traditional elite-centric administrative state and democratic mass-public participation. Three-quarters of the voters reside in the countryside, while three-quarters of Thailand wealth is found in the cities, particularly Bangkok. This has meant that for a very long time, the elite-centric Bangkok has ruled the country to its benefit with the help of the military, the technocrats and the much-needed backing of the monarchy, which is the real referee of Thai political system. Because of these issues, the Thai political system remains a democracy in transition, which seems to remain just a step away from falling back into authoritarianism. Thai people are at the heart of Thailand democratic consolidation; yet, it remains unclear whether their democratic attitudes are strong enough to keep democracy safe and continue making progress toward democratic consolidation.

Participation in elections in the most decisive means through which citizens take part in their country's political system; it is a direct, powerful and time-efficient way people have to convey their approval or disapproval of the government. In fact, elections institutionalize mass participation in the governing process, and for a large majority of citizens, voting is the only form of political participation they engage in. Social scientists have long attached a high degree of significance to voting ranging from the act of casting the ballot to the voting turnout rates. News reports invariably cite voting statistics as a benchmark of democracy; this is not surprising since elections represent an institutionalized link between citizens and the state, and serve as the basic form of political participation for citizens. Consequently, the role of elections in a democracy can be appreciated from an institutional and procedural point of view. Elections allow voters to choose their representatives and government leaders. Elections legitimize a government and its right to govern. Elections are the institutionalized way to influence government policies, and elections are one of the most convenient ways for citizens to maximize their expressive benefit. In their seven-country study, Verba, Nye and Kim observed that the combination of low information about citizens' preferences and high pressure on leaders with broad outcomes is what gives voting its unique characteristic as a blunt but powerful instrument of control over the government without requiring much initiative. Voting allows citizens directly to express differing opinions and visions for society through their choice of representative and is also the simplest form of political participation with a relatively low-opportunity cost. In Thailand, elections are a regular feature of politics even though they may not fulfill functions laid out in democratic theory, as discussed in Chapter 3.

Elections matter to how Thai citizens feel about authoritarian and democratic political systems. Among citizens who see elections as "a waste of time", 26 percent have strong authoritarian affective support; this proportion increases up to 49 percent among those who see elections as an "opportunity for patronage". However, the proportion of those who have strong authoritarian affective support drops to 35 percent for those who see elections as an "opportunity for democratic participation". Furthermore, almost equal shares of respondents who see elections either as "an opportunity for democratic participation" (i.e. 16 percent) or as "a waste of time" (i.e. 15 percent) have strong democratic affective support, whereas only 7 percent of respondents among those who see elections as "an opportunity for patronage" have strong democratic affective support. Regression results strengthen these findings and show that respondents who consider elections as "an opportunity for patronage" are 5 times more likely to show authoritarian affective support, whereas those who see elections as "an opportunity for democratic participation" are 1.3 times more likely to have authoritarian affective support. These results speak to high concentrations of cynics among those who support democracy and deny authoritarian arrangements, and strengthens the possibility of a disconnect between democracy in principle (i.e. elections are important) and democracy in practice (i.e. who elections are relevant for).

Pessimistic views of the country's economy have a strong impact on citizens with strong authoritarian affective support. In fact, economic pessimists are 3.2 times more likely to have strong authoritarian affective support. This finding indicates that a positive perception of the economy does not influence citizens' democratic attitudes as much as it does for authoritarian attitudes, which in turn suggests that commitment to democracy might not rise or fall according to how citizens perceived their country's economy to be performing. Finally, citizens who reside in rural areas are 2 times more likely to have democratic affective support, whereas respondents who live Bangkok have a higher likelihood of having authoritarian affective support. These findings suggest that urbanization does not necessarily play a critical role in shaping respondents democratic affective support, which is a sharp contrast from was modernization theory argues.

These results are telling of the need for Thailand to find a way to reconcile the relevance of the monarchy with the demand for democracy for the country to become fully democratic. The political developments of the last ten years seem to suggest that Thailand cannot escape the challenge of having the monarchy squarely within the constitution of an emerging democracy. At issue are two conflicting sources of legitimacy: the moral authority of a monarchy-centered political order and the mandate of voters-centered democratic rule. In Thailand, the upper echelons of society play a key role in determining the country's political and democratic agenda. From the end of the absolute monarchy and the introduction of democracy in 1932, the power of the people in the form of an elected representative parliament was supposed to replace the centralized political rule of the King. This constitutional development was to take place in three stages. The first stage was the period of military conquest, followed by a stage of political tutelage before reaching the final stage of a full constitutional government. Although the monarchy remained intact, the leaders of the 1932 coup introduced Western style institutions to the Thai political system, including the establishment of political parties, a parliament, a cabinet headed by a prime minister and a free press. From an institutional point of view, it appeared that power had indeed been transferred from the centralized monarchy to include a larger percentage of the population. However, nothing had really changed. The name of the political structure may have changed but political power remained in the hands of select few and the masses remained in the periphery. Although the constitutional monarchy did introduce new players to the political arena, they were drawn from the same pool of urban-based elites.

The 1932 coup may have replaced an absolutist monarch with a constitutional monarch and a parliament, but the necessary parallel evolution from being a subject of the King to a citizen of a nation did not take place. The law may officially sanction democratic institutions, however, democratic ideals have yet to be fully internalized and appreciated by the majority of the population, in particular the middle and lower classes. The military's political role might be decreasing, yet, at the same time, power has not been successfully transferred from the military to the masses, and the upper class continues to determine the political agenda. Both government and opposition politicians are guilty of the calculated use of democratic institutions to serve their own needs.

The rise of Thaksin and his subsequent political reincarnation through his relatives and political allies is an important example of these trends. It was fueled by a populist agenda centered on income redistribution, government activism and policy innovation aiming to strengthen the role of the masses in the democratization of Thailand. This agenda captured the hearts and minds of Thailand's rural majority and built the Thai Rak Thai Party into an unstoppable political machine. In February 2005, when his incumbent Government was returned to office with some 61 percent of the vote and won more than 75 percent of the seats in the House of Representatives, Prime Minister Thaksin had put Thailand on the world's emerging-markets map with impressive rates of economic growth, bold leadership and apparent democratic consolidation that seemed to promise a future in which Thailand would be politically stable and more effectively governed. The flip side to all this was the lengthening trail of corruption accusations and alleged abuses of power that Prime Minister Thaksin's Government was leaving behind. Critics charged Prime Minister Thaksin and his party with instituting authoritarian rule behind the cover provided by the democratic legitimacy that flows from winning elections. The Bangkok-based urban elites, sections of the private sector, the bureaucracy, the military and implicitly the Monarchy soon took Prime Minister Thaksin to task for what they saw as misrule for the purpose of graft and aggrandizement. This resulted in several years of political instability with the consequent frequent changes in government, including twice changing the entire regime, approving a new, more conservative constitution and the stirring up of nationalist fervor.

The abuse and misuse of democratic institutions has led to the recent re-runs of a democratically elected government voted to power by the majority of the country's mainly poor and less-educated voters seduced by the populist policies of the government, that is then removed by undemocratic means engineered by the elites culminating in color-coded protests in the streets of Bangkok. In this climate, fundamental political reforms are likely to be seen only at the margins, in spite of Thai citizens wanting a stake in reforming the country's political and institutional system. The Thai dilemma is one in which the urban elites and the monarchy need to broaden the political franchise and allow for the needs of democratic rule to be met in a real-life, politically acceptable and lasting Constitution.

6 Conclusions

Beliefs and perceptions about regime legitimacy have long been recognized as critical for the survival or breakdown of democracy, and to evaluate how far a political system has traveled toward democratic consolidation. This book used Indonesia, Korea and Thailand as case studies to investigate how ordinary citizens who have lived all or most of their lives under non-democratic rule transform themselves into democratic citizens and advocates of democracy.

The data of the SAIS 2011 Survey shows that democracy is very popular as an idea or set of values, with an average 80 percent of polled citizens across the three countries being able to tell "what democracy means to them" and identify the most and least important attributes of democracy. Citizens in Indonesia and Korea see democracy for its intended outcomes – e.g. freedom, liberty and rights – whereas Thais think of democracy mostly in terms of electoral and constitutional procedures. On the one hand, procedural understanding of democracy could be the result of Thailand's checkered history of democracy, which over the years, might have strengthened the value of process over that of substance in the eyes of Thai citizens. On the other, Indonesians' and Koreans' experiences with political regimes where democratic procedures were used to perpetuate the existence of non-democratic political systems might help explain their strong substance-based views of democracy.

The majority of polled citizens in Indonesia and Korea has a positive, multi-dimensional understanding of democracy, whereas for Thais democracy is mostly uni-dimensional. In general, democracy is seen as a competitive system of governance in which people have a dispositive say in how they are governed. Freedom and rights are seen as fundamental properties of democracy, even if they are not necessarily the most popular attributes of democracy in Korea and Thailand. Finally, only in Korea, a significant share of respondents (i.e. 15 percent) equate democracy with economics and consider economic growth to be as essential as political rights or civil liberties to the idea of democracy.

These findings are important because they tell that democracy as an idea is meaningful to citizens in spite of the fact that for most of their lives Indonesians, Koreans and Thais might not have experienced the kind of democracy that is described in their definitions of democracy. Only if democracy as an idea is meaningful to citizens (i.e. they know what it is), they can eventually express affective (i.e. democracy is good or bad in practice) and evaluative (i.e. in favor or against democracy in practice) support for it.

An important corollary to citizens' understanding of democracy is what causes democracy to spread across countries around the world. A popular theme in democratic literature argues that both citizens' understanding of democracy and one's country political and institutional choices could be influenced by forces originating outside a country's borders – rather than being a self-contained domestic process – and proposes various interpretations of how democratization occurs and what role citizens play in this process. If one country employs democracy-enhancing ideas, its neighbors may become more likely to adopt them as well. This may be true, but there are reasons to suspect that learning democracy may be more complicated than just discerning democratic success. Democratization processes are notoriously difficult to pin down due to the disturbances created by country regional clustering, global trends and domestic factors.

How democracy spread is an even more tantalizing question when it comes to Asian countries. In fact, since 1974, when the current wave of democratization begun, the movement toward democracy in Asia has remained limited, with only 8 countries becoming electoral democracies in the past 30 years out of more than 60 countries that have become democratic around the world.[1] For many years, Korea vacillated between parliamentary and military governments until it completed its transition from military rule to democracy with the direct presidential elections of 1987. Indonesia successfully transitioned to democracy following the fall of President Suharto in 1998. However, widespread corruption, incomplete institutional reforms and dysfunctional bureaucracy have been common features of Indonesia's progress toward democratic consolidation. Finally, even if people in Thailand are outspoken about the need for democracy to take firm roots in their country, Thailand's "stop-and-go" process toward finding a legitimate form of government, with 18 constitutions and 18 coups since 1932, remains without precedent in the annals of democracy. Yet, for all the recent progress

---

1 Freedom House. 2012 Freedom in the World Survey. www.Freedomhouse.org

and in spite of being a popular idea, democracy does not seem to take roots easily and steadily in Asia.

Democratic diffusion presupposes the idea, among others, that people in country "A" learn that country "B" has become a democracy, and that this influences mass following of democracy in country "A" presupposes that people in country "A" have an accurate or semi-accurate knowledge of country "B". Data from the SAIS 2011 Survey, however, point to the fact that Indonesians, Koreans and Thais do not recognize democratic political systems outside their own countries. In fact, across the three countries, the vast majority of respondents are sure that their own country is a democracy but seem rather unsure of whether in Asia, countries other that their own are democratic or non-democratic, with knowledge of democratic political systems being poorer than that of authoritarian ones. These results cast doubts on the theory that democracy-friendly ideas arriving from democratic neighbors such as India and the Philippines played a role in Indonesia, Korea and Thailand becoming democratic. These results are, however, consistent with evidence from early studies of political culture and political development, which discounted the ability of the public in nascent democracies to recognize democracy outside their countries.

Some scholars view democratization as the result of the ebb and flow of information at domestic, regional and global levels, this does not seem to be happening in Indonesia, Korea and Thailand, particularly at the mass levels. With large-scale political change, the decision to adopt or not adopt it is made at an institutional level, with both elite's and mass' perceptions of the relative benefits, compatibility, complexity and suitability of democracy in the local context playing a key role. In the case of Indonesia, Korea and Thailand, there may be an overall interest to catch up to the "democratic wave" among Jakarta, Seoul and Bangkok well-educated and politically knowledgeable elites, but not at the mass levels, in spite of the popularity of democracy as a political ideal. Furthermore, findings from spatial econometric analysis show that the strength with which democracy spread across Asia might have been overstated. In fact, an annual spread rate varying between 8 and 11 percent is hardly one that describes democracy "spreading like a wave". Thus, citizens' knowledge of the political regimes of neighboring countries and/or the geographic location of a country does not seem to be factors important enough to be able to influence or constrain the nature of political regimes across Asia, or the choices available to political elites in the region.

When it comes to mass sentiments about "democracy as the preferred political system to govern their countries", the attitudes displayed by respondents in Indonesia, Korea and Thailand are inchoate and do not necessarily seem to provide enough support for a democratic political system to survive and strengthen. Democratic support is a multi-dimensional phenomenon, with one dimension involving the development of favorable orientations toward democratic ideals while another one pertains to develop support for democratic institutions and practices. Trends for citizens' support for authoritarian or democratic forms of government show that rejection of authoritarianism while supporting democracy seems not to be happening across the three countries. For every Indonesian in favor of having a democratic regime there are two who would prefer an authoritarian one. In Thailand, the same ratio is 1 to 3, and in Korea is 1 to 4. Moreover, across these countries between 45 and 55 percent of respondents seem to harbor concurrent appreciations for authoritarian and democratic political systems. Citizens with little experience of and limited sophistication concerning democratic politics may be uncertain whether democracy or authoritarianism offers the best solution to the problems facing their countries. Because of this, citizens who are new to democracy often embrace both democracy and authoritarianism. These findings suggest that support for democracy in Indonesia, Korea and Thailand "could be a mile wide and an inch deep" per Gibson's apt description of the democratic reality in Eastern European countries and the former Soviet Union in the 1990s.

Citizens' affective democratic support and democratic cognitive skills should not be analyzed in isolation one from the other, but for their interrelation as democratic cognitive skills play a role in whether a links develops between affective support and satisfaction with democracy as a political system. It is presumed that citizens who do not understand democracy will probably be indifferent to whether democracy is good or bad for their country and to how democracy performs. However, if citizens understand democracy as an idea/set of values, it is probable that they would want their country's political regime to conform to that idea, and would want to be supportive of it in practice. Findings from the SAIS 2000 and 2011 Surveys show that there is a relatively large share of respondents whose affective support for democracy seems inchoate in spite of a very strong cognitive support for democracy. This coupled with the fact that another third of respondents who, across the three countries, show strong affective support for authoritarianism, suggest that cognitive and affective support for democracy do not go hand in hand in Indonesia, Korea and Thailand, and this reality could became a significant obstacle to lasting democratic consolidation in any of the three countries.

Overall, citizens' understanding and support of democracy in Indonesia, Korea and Thailand both as an idea and a political regime appear to be rooted in what citizens learn from their experience about what democracy is and what it does at home. To different extents, these findings are consistent with Almond and Verba's arguments that, at country-level, cross-national differences in individual attitudes toward democracy result from long-standing differences in norms and values, and economic orientations that are transmitted through socialization across generations. This approach predicts that popular understanding of a particular political system (e.g. democracy) would be mostly shaped by the individuals' personal norms and values.

Country-specific combinations of factors influence citizens' affective support for democracy, and their overlap across Indonesia, Korea and Thailand is limited to individual perception of their countries' economic outlook. Asia has long been regarded as a nearly perfect test ground for the relationship between democratization and economic development. In many Asian countries, the initial economic development took place under the leadership of authoritarian regimes. Yet, there is consensus that the economic performance and achievements of the successor democratic governments fare well when compared with what their predecessors achieved. This is probably why the influence of economics is considerably less than that of other relevant variables, thus suggesting that citizens' commitment to democracy may be less a function of what it does for the economy than of how democracy itself is experienced. This finding supports Linz's and Stepan's arguments that citizens are able to distinguish between "a basket of economic goods (which may be deteriorating) and a basket of political goods (which may be improving)".[2] Commitment to democracy seems to be insulated from the influence of economics, and mass support for democracy does not seem to be eroded by occasional or recurrent economic shocks. The argument that, at some point, citizens will abandon democracy because it has failed to produce satisfactory economic results and/or that alternative authoritarian political arrangements are believed to yield better economic results does not seem to apply, particularly to Indonesia and Thailand. In the case of Korea, however, respondents' changes in disposable income – and not their perception of the country' overall economic outlook – seem to matter more, relatively speaking, than in any of the other countries vis-à-vis their ability to define democracy and their affective support for democratic regimes. These findings signal that democracy in Korea is not insulated from personal economic experiences and aspirations as much it appears to be in Indonesia and Thailand. This is important and possibly a result of the fact that the years of democratic consolidation saw widening socio-economic polarization and inequality with the country labor market becoming increasingly fragmented and stratified.

---

2   Juan Linz and Alfred Stepan. 1996. Problems of Democratic Transition and Consolidation: Southern Europe, South America and Post-Communist Europe. Baltimore, MD: Johns Hopkins University Press.

Unexpectedly, non-electoral forms of participation are not key for citizens' cognitive and affective support of democracy in Indonesia, Korea and Thailand. In addition to select governments and parliaments, citizens should engage in political and civic activities between the infrequent elections. Regardless of whether people write letters, sign petitions, go to election meetings, or join political and non-political organizations, democracy requires an independent civil society able to enjoy civil and political rights necessary to guard against possible excesses of the government. It is from these groups and their activities that political leaders understand citizens' political mood and aspirations in-between elections. By channeling the demands and concerns of citizens to the state, interest groups help ensure accountability and transparency, and in doing so, they strengthen the country's democracy. These forces, however, seem to be generally absent from Indonesia, Korea and Thailand, where patron–client groups both contest elections and contend in-between elections. Still, membership in civil society organizations appears to be growing (except in Korea), but the proportion of the population participating in both civil society and in politics between elections remains relatively small. All in all, civil society is small, vertically rather than horizontally structured, and does not necessarily assemble citizens with similar socio-economic interests or ideological views.

Overall, the findings from the SAIS 2000 and 2011 Surveys and discussion in the chapters of this book point to the fact that democracy seems to survive in Indonesia, Korea and Thailand not because of citizens' coherent cognitive and affective support for democracy both as an idea and as a political regime but because there seem to be a tacit consensus that, with all of its imperfections, democracy remains the best way forward. This reality, although not necessarily positive, is an improvement over the authoritarian governments that governed Indonesia, Korea and Thailand in the not so distant past.

Much of mass' attitudes about democracy remain a work in progress. This places a heavy burden on leaders and the educated elites for them to nurture and foster consensus on democracy and democratic practices across their societies. For democracy to be sustained in Indonesia, Korea and Thailand, an appropriate mix of mass sentiments and democratic processes like elections, non-electoral participation and civil society must be in place, together with responsible elites and capable pro-democratic leaders. Unfortunately, because of all these requirements and the existing incoherent public sentiments about democracy as a political system, democratic consolidation across these three countries continues to be a humbling work in progress, with little lasting success to show for to date.

Annex 1: the 2000 and 2011 SAIS Surveys

The SAIS 2000 Survey

The SAIS 2000 Survey was the first opinion survey designed by the SAIS Southeast Asia Studies Program to investigate the 1997 East Asian financial crisis as a possible cause of broad social, economic and political changes that might alter the development trajectory of Indonesia, the Philippines, Korea and Thailand. The survey focused only on the capital cities of Jakarta, Manila, Seoul and Bangkok, had a sampling size of 300 individuals per capital city and used a semi-original,[1] 12-modules questionnaire, which comprised 135 questions, 10 percent of which were open-ended. The target population of the SAIS 2000 Survey had not participated in any survey in the six months prior to the survey. AC Nielsen implemented the survey, and the field-work was divided in two phases: the pre-test phase and the implementation phase. The 2000 Survey was pre-tested in each capital, between January and February 2000, through a limited number of pre-test interviews ranging between 10 and 15, in each capital; the implementation phase took place between March and April 2000; the interviews were conducted face to face and lasted approximately 1.5 hours.

The SAIS 2000 Survey used a stratified random sampling framework, which included the following specifications:

a. AC Nielsen classified each Primary Sampling Unit (PSU) in each of the four countries as A, B, C, D or E according to the monthly household income level and the general characteristics of the specific neighborhood where PSUs were located.

---

1 Several of the questions included in the SAIS 2000 Socio-economic Survey came from the World Value Survey, and they were used in their original form or slightly modified to fit the specific context of the SAIS 2000 survey.

b. Jakarta included more exact sampling units than Seoul. In Jakarta, a PSU was composed of 50 households; to align the random sampling for Jakarta as closely as possible to the one for Bangkok or Seoul, AC Nielsen statisticians suggested generating three interviews per PSU. In Bangkok, the sample population was adjusted for age and gender; PSU included 100 households, and respondents were randomly selected from each household using the Keish grid method.[2] The margin of error in the Bangkok 2000 sample size was approximately 5.7 percent.[3]
c. In Seoul, the number of households per PSU (i.e. the dong[4]) was not standardized and could vary significantly among PSUs. To have the same clustering of households across the four countries, AC Nielsen counted the number of households in randomly selected dongs, then sub-divided the results into several areas so that each area contained 100 households, and six interviews could be generated per each PSU.

The SAIS 2011 Survey

The 2011 SAIS Survey is a national-level opinion survey, which targeted Indonesia, the Philippines, Korea and Thailand, with a total sampling size of 4,000 individuals. To ensure consistency with the SAIS 2000 Survey, the 2011 survey included a capital city sample of 300 individuals and used an updated version of the questionnaire used for the 2000 survey. As in 2000, AC Nielsen implemented the surveys across the four countries, and the fieldwork was divided in two phases: the pre-test phase and the implementation phase. The 2011 survey was pre-tested in each country only at capital-level in January 2011, through a limited number of pre-test interviews, which ranged between 10 and 15 interviews. The implementation

---

2   The Keish grid method is a widely used technique in survey research, by which interviewers who have been issued with a sample of household addresses can then sample individuals on the doorstep, by following simple and rigorous rules for selecting one person to interview from among household residents. The technique involves constructing a list of eligible individuals at a particular address, ordered by age, and then selecting according to the serial number of the address itself. The system is devised so that all individuals in a household have an equal chance of selection. Its major difficulty is that the individual who supplies the household listing is often not the one to be interviewed.
3   The margin of error equals $1.96[(\sqrt{pq})/(\sqrt{300})]$ where $q = (1 - p)$. The margin of error is maximized when $p = 5$; the sample size would have to increase by about 100 respondents to reduce the margin of error by 1 percent.
4   In Korea, the dong is the lowest administrative unit of districts and of those cities which are not divided into wards. The primary division of a dong is the "tong"; divisions at the "tong" level (and below) are seldom used in daily life. Some populous dong are subdivided into "ga", which do not constitute an administrative unit but only exist for use in addresses.

phase took place between February and June 2011, with interviews conducted face to face at national and capital level, with each interview lasting approximately 1.5 hours.

The SAIS 2011 Survey used a stratified random sampling framework, which included the following specifications:

a. Respondents were males and females of voting age for national election. For Indonesia the voting age is 17 years old, for Thailand it is 18 years old, and for Korea it is 19 years old. Participating respondents were from all socio-economic backgrounds and from both urban and rural areas reflective of the national population.
b. Indonesia had a success rate of 63 percent and a refusal rate of 6 percent. Korea had a success rate of 45 percent and a refusal rate of 35 percent. Thailand had a success rate of 41 percent and a refusal rate of 3 percent. The AC Nielsen Team for Thailand clarified that the refusal rate was in line with that of similar other studies Nielsen conducted over the same period of time and not impacted by the upcoming national elections of June 2011 or the political turbulence of 2010.
c. The sampling methodology across countries followed four phases. Phase 1 dealt with the selection of the PSUs; Phase 2 with the selection of Secondary Sampling Units (SSU); Phase 3 focused on the selection of the household. For each sampled area map, a random start number was specified; this was a randomly generated number, which refers to the house from the starting point where first interview will be attempted. Phase 4 dealt with the selection of respondents using a probability grid. Similar to the 2000 survey, the selection of target respondents within a household was done through the Keish grid method. Valid number of callbacks followed AC Nielsen's local standards for random sampling methodology. The number of interviews per sampling unit varied per country, according to Nielsen's local standards. For Korea and Thailand, the AC Nielsen teams conducted 10 interviews per sampling unit. In Indonesia, AC Nielsen local standards required 6 interviews per sampling unit. Finally, weights have been applied to the data given the size capital-city sampling (n = 300) and the need to reflect it back to the actual population distribution.
d. The Korean administrative units (in descending order of size) include: i) Si/Do (Seoul); ii) Si/Gun/Gu-Eup/Myun/Dong; iii) Tong/Ban/Li (Tong and Ban are used for urban areas, and Li is used for rural areas). The AC Nielsen Korean team divided Korean population into clusters by the Si/Do of their residence. Next, the AC Nielsen team looked at the share of the total Korean population each Si/Do represented and selected the population sample to be potentially interviewed from each

Si/Do proportional to each Si/Do's share of the total Korean population. That is, if the residents of a Si/Do equaled 10 percent of the Korean population, the sample drawn from that Si/Do would represent 10 percent of the total national sample for Korea for the 2011 Survey. The population in each Si/Do was then divided into smaller clusters by Si/Gun/Gu. The Nielsen team looked at the share of the total Si/Do population each Si/Gun/Gu in the Si/Do represented and made the sample selected from each Si/Gun/Gu proportional to each Si/Gun/Gu's share of the Si/Dos total population. As for the Quota Selection, the population within each Si/Gun/Gu was clustered by the Eup/Myun/Dong in which they reside; then a quota random sample of the Eup/Myun/Dong was selected from each Si/Gun/Gu. That is, a large Si/Gun/Gu with a large population would have a greater number of Eup/Myun/Dong randomly selected than a smaller Si/Gun/Gu with a smaller population. Within each selected Eup/Myun/Dong, Tong/Ban/Li were randomly selected and 15 interviews were conducted within each Tong/Ban/Li.[5] Within each Tong/Ban/Li both the households and the respondents to be interviewed, within each household, were randomly selected.

KOREA

Region/Province	Total	Urban	Rural
Seoul	300	300	0
Pusan/Ulsan/Gyeognam	114	91	23
Daegu/Gyeongbuk	77	54	23
Inchun/Gyonggi	183	156	27
Gwangju/Jeonbuk/Jeonnam	74	50	24
Daejun/Chungbuk/Chungnam	72	45	27
Gangwon/Jeju	30	19	11
TOTAL	**850**	**715**	**135**

e. Indonesia administrative units include *kabupatens, kecamatans* and *desas*; the lists of all the strata divisions of these administrative units are publicly available through central and local government agencies.

5 Example: So if "Si/Gun/Gu a" is allocated a quota of 100 respondents for this study: 7 Eup/Myun/Dong will be selected randomly from "Si/Gun/Gu a"; 7 Tong/Ban/Li are randomly selected from each of the selected Eup/Myun/Dong; 15 respondent interviews are to be conducted in each of the selected Tong/Ban/Lis from "Si/Gun/Gu a sampling summary for "Si/Gun/Gu a": 7 Eup/Myun/Dong; 7 Tong/Ban/Lis; 100 total respondents interviewed.

Within each administrative unit, the population is divided into neighborhood units comprising approximately 40–50 households; these population sub-divisions are called *Rukun Tetanggas* (R. T.). Within any area, the Indonesia Nielsen team selected a sample frame through a fixed-interval selection method from the list of R. T. made available by the local governments. Specifically, based on the regular R. T. census, which is conducted every two years, AC Nielsen statisticians selected 1000 R. T., which were mapped to identify roads, major buildings, houses and other main physical features, and also given a score, from 1 to 10, based on these physical characteristics; then, a list of at least 50 households was developed within each selected R. T. If the R. T. surveyed was not deemed feasible for the purpose of the survey, a substitute R. T. would have been selected within the same kecamatan and the same R. T. score, based on various physical features of the R. T.[6]

INDONESIA

Region/Province	Total	Urban	Rural
Sumatera (Sumatera Utara/Sumatera Selatan/Riau/Lampung)	153	62	91
Java (DKI Jakarta, Jawa Barat. Jawa Tengah, DI Yogyakarta, Jawa Timur, Banten)	961	652	309
Bali + Nusa Tenggara (Bali, Nusa Tenggara Bara)	42	21	21
Kalimantan (Kalimantan Barat, Kalimantan Timur)	38	16	22
Sulawesi (Sulawesi Utara, Sulawesi Selatan)	56	20	36
TOTAL	**1250**	**771**	**479**

f. In Thailand, for the Greater Bangkok Metropolitan Region (GBMR), the AC Nielsen team first selected and grouped 80 PSUs according to monthly household income level and the general characteristics of the neighborhood where PSUs were located; then, households were randomly selected within any one PSU. As for rural areas, target districts within provinces were selected first and then two sub-districts

---

6 AC Nielsen estimates and scores of the number of R. T. to be used for a specific project are generally based on response rates from previous projects of a similar kind and on the standard response rate. If the actual response rate is lower than target response rate after callback, additional PSUs are selected with systematic random sampling to achieve the agreed target number of respondents.

(i.e. *tambon*) were selected within each district, and three villages within each sub-district for interviews.

THAILAND

Region/Province	Total	Urban	Rural
Bangkok	300	300	0
North (Changmai/Pitsanulok)	150	36	114
Northeastern (Khonkaen/Ubonratchatani)	150	34	116
Central (Chonburi/ Nakornsawan)	150	36	114
South (Songkhla/ Suratthani)	150	36	114
TOTAL	**900**	**442**	**458**

Annex 2: statistical and spatial econometric analyses

1. Statistical analysis

The data that inform this book benefitted from:

- Cross-tabular analysis that has been used to assess the relevance of the observations emerging from the data of the 2000 and 2011 SAIS surveys. The cross-tabulations use a 0.05 level of significance. The robustness of any cross-tabular association is measured using Theil's U.
- Factor and discriminant analysis has been used to assess the feasibility and reliability of a variety of indexes and scales, and results of cross-tabulations.
- Logistic regression analysis was used to assess the impact of a number of factors on the respondents' awareness of democracy and democratic or authoritarian attitudes. The decision to use binary or multinomial logit regressions was deemed more appropriate than ordered logit because the majority of responses to the SAIS 2000 and 2011 Surveys were not ordinal in nature. The multinomial logit regression model allows to predict the probabilities of the different possible outcomes of a categorically distributed dependent variable, given a set of independent variables (which may be binary valued, categorical valued, etc.); this feature allows to capture as much variation as possible among responses and respondents rather than simply capturing the direction of the relationship. Furthermore, the choice of logistic regressions simplifies the analysis of the relationship between independent and dependent variables as it allows seeing how the relationships are determined and reveals impacts for each of the categories of the dependent variables without burdening the regression with controls like those usually used in liner regressions.

Indonesia democratic cognitive skills

The dependent variable for "democratic cognitive skills" was computed, recoding the original response to Question 81: "What does democracy mean to you?" The new variable assigns a value of "0" to respondents who did not offer a definition of democracy, or answered "Do not know" or "Can't say", whereas a value of 1 is assigned to respondents who offered a definition of democracy as an answer to Question 81. The following independent variables were used in the cross-tabulations:

Age; Gender; Education; Urban and Rural Status; Exposure to Media; Media Trust; Modern Opinion Leaders; Traditional Advisors, Modern; Opinion-Leaders and Traditional Advisors; Traditional Advisor/Advisee; Individual Perception of Indonesia Macro-economic Outlook; Retrospective, Current and Prospective Views of Indonesia Macro-economic Outlook; Individual Consumption of Consumer Goods; Individual Ownership of Durable Goods; Social Capital Formation; Dispute Resolution; Propensity to Violence; Membership in Civil Society Organizations; Interest in Politics; Knowledge of Politics; Knowledge of Asian Authoritarian Systems; Knowledge of Asian Democratic Systems; Membership/Affiliation with Political Parties; Participation in Activities of Political Parties, regardless of membership or affiliation; Non-electoral Participation; Attitudes toward Elections; Voting in Presidential Elections; Voting in Parliamentary Elections; Voting in Local Elections; Preferences for Authoritarian, Technocratic, Military or Democratic Regimes to Govern Indonesia.

Annex 2.1. Indonesia 2011 summary results for correlations and significance of associations for respondents' democratic cognitive skills

	Pearson Chi Square	Theil's U
Maintain significance at the 0.05 level with a Theil's U above 15 percent		
Age	0.000	0.057
Gender	0.000	0.018
Urban or Rural Status	0.000	0.049
Education	0.000	0.050
Modern Opinion Leader and Traditional Advisors	0.000	0.055
Traditional Advisor	0.000	0.027
Interest in Politics	0.000	0.022
Political Knowledge	0.000	0.030
Individual Perception of ID Macro-economic Outlook	0.000	0.040
Retrospective Perception of ID Macro-economic Outlook	0.001	0.015
Current Perception of ID Macro-economic Outlook	0.000	0.017
Prospective Perception of ID Macro-economic Outlook	0.000	0.015
Membership/Affiliation with Political Parties	0.000	0.017
Participation in Political Parties Activities	0.000	0.015
Maintain significance at the 0.05 level with a Theil's U below 15 percent		
Trust in the Media	0.000	0.010
Exposure to Media	0.005	0.012
Individual Consumption of Consumer Goods	0.006	0.014
CSOs Participation	0.001	0.010
NEP	0.005	0.010
Fail to maintain significance at the 0.05 level		
Social Capital Formation		
Ownership of Durable Goods		
Modern Opinion Leaders		
Traditional Advisor/Advisee		
Dispute Resolution		
Non-electoral Participation		
Voting in Presidential Elections		
Voting in Parliamentary Elections		
Voting in Local Election		

Annex 2.2. Indonesia 2011 summary results for logistic regression model for respondents' democratic cognitive skills

	B	SE	Sig	Exp(B)
Age				
17–29	1.333	.321	.000	4.091
30–39	1.219	.338	.000	3.384
40–49	1.161	.337	.001	3.193
50–59	.599	.335	.074	1.821
60 and Up	.489	.331	.085	1.109
Gender				
Male	.721	.255	.002	2.037
Female	.654	.215	.000	1.947
Urbanity				
Capital City	1.876	.521	.000	6.527
Urban Non-capital	.256	.233	.239	1.291
Rural	.654	.374	.194	.945
Individual perception of ID macro-economic outlook				
Optimistic	−1.187	.269	.000	.275
Pessimistic	−1.094	.239	.195	.475
Individual consumption of consumer goods				
Same	.342	.290	.239	1.407
Mixed	.331	.363	.362	1.393
Declined	1.467	.411	.000	4.338
Less	.623	.321	.052	1.865
Never Bought	.597	.457	.097	1.675
Social capital formation				
Group Response	−.672	.221	.002	.510
Non-group Response	−.514	.319	.001	.713
Dispute resolution				
Formal Mechanism	.618	.174	.000	1.854
Informal Mechanisms	.600	.197	.000	1.215
Political knowledge				
No to Low Knowledge	−.769	.227	.001	.463
Medium-to-High Knowledge	−.650	.210	.000	.570

Regression model reference category: Respondents' Democratic Cognitive Skills
Chi Square: 167.21
N = 1154
Cox and Snell: 14.1%
Nagelkerke: 29.8%

Korea democratic cognitive skills

Annex 2.3. Korea 2011 summary results for correlations and significance of associations for democratic cognitive skills

	Pearson Chi Square	Theil's U
Maintain significance at the 0.05 level, with a Theil's U equal or above 15 percent		
Age	0.009	0.024
Education	0.040	0.016
Maintain significance at the 0.05 level, with a Theil's U below 15 percent		
Urban and Rural Status	0.045	0.009
Gender	0.037	0.008
Social Capital Formation	0.015	0.010
Dispute Resolution	0.020	0.005
Fail to maintain significance at the 0.05 level		
Media Exposure	0.774	
Trust in the Media	0.427	
Modern Opinion Leader	0.760	
Traditional Advisor	0.135	
Participation in CSOs	0.975	
Traditional Advisor and Modern Opinion Leader	0.369	
Individual Perception of SK Macro-economic Outlook	0.421	
Individual Consumption of Consumer Goods	0.222	
Individual Ownership of Durable Goods	0.158	
Interest in Politics	0.496	
Individual Perception of SK Macro-economic Outlook	0.165	
Retrospective View of SK Macro-economic Outlook	0.356	
Current View of SK Macro-economic Outlook	0.568	
Prospective View of SK Macro-economic Outlook	0.459	
Political Knowledge	0.545	
Political Party Membership	0.083	
Participation in Political Party Activities	0.207	
NEP	0.800	
Attitudes toward Elections	0.114	
Voting in Presidential Elections	0.235	
Voting in Parliamentary Elections	0.345	
Voting in Local Elections	0.269	

Annex 2.4. Korea 2011 logistic regression model for predictors of citizens' democratic cognitive skills

	B	SE	Sig	Exp(B)
Education				
Secondary Education	.303	.501	.004	1.475
University Level Education	.632	.495	.026	2.455
Individual consumption of consumers' goods				
More or the Same	.654	.419	.006	1.654
Mixed	1.137	.275	.001	3.574
Declined	1.674	.630	.016	2.680
Severely Declined	.915	.210	.000	2.010
Stop Buying or Never Bought	.752	.459	.008	1.395

Regression model reference category: Democratic Cognitive Skills
Chi Square: 65.579
Significance Level = 0.05
N = 809
Cox and Snell R^2: 4.9%
Nagelkerke R^2: 17.5%

Thailand democratic cognitive skills

Annex 2.5. Thailand 2011 summary results for correlations and association of significance for democratic cognitive skills

	Pearson Chi Square	Theil's U
Maintain significance at the 0.05 level, with Theil's U equal or above 15 percent		
Media Exposure	0.019	0.017
Individual Consumption of Consumer Goods	0.000	0.024
Political Knowledge	0.001	0.021
Maintain significance at the 0.05 level, with Theil's U below 15 percent		
Participation in CSOs	0.006	0.014
Modern Opinion Leader	0.037	0.008
Social Capital Formation	0.015	0.010
Dispute Resolution	0.020	0.005
Fail to maintain significance at the 0.05 level		
Age	0.264	
Gender	0.255	
Urban and Rural Status	0.483	
Education	0.063	
Media Trust	0.420	
Traditional Advisor	0.919	
Traditional Advisor and Advisee	0.899	
Traditional Advisor and Modern Opinion Leader	0.267	
Individual Ownership of Durable Goods	0.238	
Interest in Politics	0.125	
Individual Perception of TH Macro-economic Outlook	0.234	
Retrospective View of TH Macro-economic Outlook	0.128	
Current View of TH Macro-economic Outlook	0.238	
Prospective View of TH Macro-economic Outlook	0.349	
NEP	0.149	
Attitudes toward Elections	0.248	
Political Party Membership	0.431	
Participation in Political Party Activities	0.169	
Voting in National Elections	0.431	
Voting in Local Elections	0.89	

Annex 2.6. Thailand 2011 summary results for the logistic regression model for respondents' democratic cognitive skills

	B	SE	Sig	Exp(B)
Individual consumption of consumers' goods				
More or the Same	−.978	.625	.118	.376
Mixed	−1.524	.618	.014	.218
Declining	−1.676	.591	.005	.187
Severely Declining	−.171	.801	.831	.185
Never Bought	−.204	.654	.391	.953
CSOs participation				
No Participation	−1.175	.543	.030	.309
Low Participation	−1.640	.548	.003	.194
Medium-to-High Participation	−1.475	.498	.045	.185

Regression model reference category: Democratic Cognitive Skills
Chi Square: 27.201
N = 890
Cox and Snell R^2: 6.2%
Nagelkerke R^2: 15.3%

Indonesia democracy as an outcome or as a process

Annex 2.7. Indonesia 2011 summary results for correlations and significance of associations for democracy as a process or as an outcome

	Pearson Chi Square	Theil's U
Maintain significance at the 0.05 level with Theil's U values below 15 percent		
Urban or Rural Status	0.023	0.006
Social Capital Formation	0.004	0.007
Political Knowledge	0.000	0.013
Fail to maintain significance at the 0.05 level		
Age	0.235	
Gender	0.689	
Education	0.436	
Individual Perception of ID Macro-economic Outlook	0.599	
Retrospective Perception of ID Macro-economic Outlook	0.468	
Current Perception of ID Macro-economic Outlook	0.460	
Prospective Perception of ID Macro-economic Outlook	0.436	
Membership/Affiliation with Political Parties	0.724	
Participation in Political Parties Activities	0.074	
Trust in the Media	0.929	
Exposure to Media	0.101	
Individual Consumption of Consumer Goods	0.321	
CSOs Participation	0.214	
NEP	0.982	
Ownership of Durable Goods	0.753	
Modern Opinion Leaders	0.894	
Dispute Resolution	0.738	
Traditional Advisor	0.684	
Modern Opinion Leader/Traditional Advisor	0.961	
Interest in Politics	0.334	
Traditional Advisor/Advisee	0.134	
Voting in Presidential Elections	0.458	
Voting in Parliamentary Elections	0.764	
Voting in Local Elections	0.456	
Individual Ownership of Durable Goods	0.359	

Annex 2.8. Indonesia 2011 summary results for the logistic regression model for democracy as a process or an outcome

	B	SE	Sig	Exp(B)
Political knowledge				
No to Low Knowledge	.630	.166	.000	1.882
Medium-to-High Knowledge	.510	.175	.001	2.010
Social capital formation				
Group Response	−.350	.152	.021	.705
Non-group Response	−.456	.215	.011	.750

Regression model reference category: Substantive View of Democracy
Chi Square: 19.728
N = 1050
Cox and Snell R^2: 24%
Nagelkerke R^2 : 32%

Korea democracy as a process or as an outcome

Annex 2.9. Korea 2011 summary results for correlations and significance of associations for democracy as a process or as an outcome

	Pearson Chi Square	Theil's U
Maintain significance at the 0.05 level, with a Theil's U equal or above 15 percent		
Modern Opinion Leader	0.001	0.021
Non-electoral Participation	0.000	0.037
Maintain significance at the 0.05 level, with a Theil's U below 15 percent		
Gender	0.018	0.006
Individual Consumption of Consumer Goods	0.034	0.014
Affiliation/Participation in Civil Society Organizations	0.023	0.010
Affiliation with Political Parties	0.010	0.008
Fail to maintain significance at the 0.05 level		
Age	0.189	
Urbanity	0.340	
Media Exposure	0.072	
Trust in the Media	0.473	
Traditional Advisor	0.665	
Individual Ownership of Durable Goods	0.375	
Interest in Politics	0.496	
Individual Perception of SK Macro-economic Outlook	0.960	
Retrospective View of SK Macro-economic Outlook	0.564	
Current View of SK Macro-economic Outlook	0.653	
Prospective View of SK Macro-economic Outlook	0.876	
Social Capital Formation	0.133	
Political Knowledge	0.290	
Dispute Resolution	0.152	
Participation in Pol. Party Activities, Regardless of Membership	0.625	
Attitudes toward Elections	0.472	
Voting in Presidential Elections	0.580	
Voting in Parliamentary Elections	0.653	
Voting in Local Elections	0.348	
Education	0.457	
Traditional Advisor/Advisee	0.245	
Modern Opinion Leader and Traditional Advisor	0.334	

Annex 2.10. Korea 2011 summary results for logistic regression model for democracy as a process or an outcome

	B	SE	Sig	Exp(B)
Non-electoral participation				
No NEP	.833	.328	.011	2.299
Low NEP	−.176	.284	.536	.839
Medium–to-High NEP	.655	.315	.007	1.244

Regression model reference category: Democracy an Outcome
Chi Square: 38.060
Significance Level = 0.05
N = 815
Cox and Snell R^2: 37%
Nagelkerke R^2: 53%

Thailand democracy as a process or as an outcome

Annex 2.11. Thailand 2011 summary results for correlations and significance of associations for democracy as a process or as an outcome

	Pearson Chi Square	Theil's U
Maintain significance at the 0.05 level, with a Theil's U equal or above 15 percent		
Age	0.018	0.015
Modern Opinion Leader	0.000	0.017
Individual Consumption of Consumer Goods	0.010	0.017
CSOs Membership and Participation	0.002	0.016
Participation in Political Party Activities	0.000	0.032
Non-electoral Participation	0.000	0.023
Maintain significance at the 0.05 level, with a Theil's U below 15 percent		
Urban and Rural Status	0.026	0.009
Media Exposure	0.023	0.012
Social Capital Formation	0.039	0.006
Dispute Resolution	0.004	0.011
Political Knowledge	0.040	0.005
Attitudes toward Elections	0.016	0.011
Fail to maintain significance at the 0.05 level		
Gender	0.148	
Education	0.351	
Interest in Politics	0.135	
Trust in the Media	0.690	
Traditional Advisor	0.600	
Individual Ownership of Durable Goods	0.355	
Individual Perception of TH Macro-economic Outlook	0.757	
Retrospective View of SK Macro-economic Outlook	0.164	
Current View of SK Macro-economic Outlook	0.753	
Prospective View of SK Macro-economic Outlook	0.826	
Voting in Presidential Elections	0.180	
Voting in Parliamentary Elections	0.453	
Voting in Local Elections	0.248	
Traditional Advisor/Advisee	0.145	
Modern Opinion Leader and Traditional Advisor	0.234	

Annex 2.12. Thailand 2011 summary results for logistic regression model for democracy as a process or as an outcome

	B	SE	Sig	Exp(B)
Attitudes toward Elections				
Elections Are a Waste of Time	.956	.398	.016	2.602
Elections Are an Exercise in Patronage	.964	.264	.000	2.621
Elections Are an Opportunity for Democratic Participation	.865	.195	.000	2.775
CSO Membership/Participation				
No Membership/Participation in CSOs	.574	.398	.041	1.775
Low Membership/Participation in CSOs	−.595	.264	.597	.856
Medium-to-High Membership/Participation in CSOs	.459	.216	.045	1.215

Regression model reference category: Procedural View of Democracy
Chi Square: 38.068
Significance Level = 0.05
N = 871
Cox and Snell R^2: 10.3%
Nagelkerke R^2: 19.1%

Indonesia democratic and authoritarian affective support

Annex 2.13. Indonesia 2011 democracy scale raw scores

		Frequency	Percentage	Cumulative Percentage
Raw Scores	.00	49	3.8	3.8
	4.00	12	.9	4.7
	5.00	4	.3	5.0
	6.00	3	.3	5.3
	7.00	29	2.2	7.5
	8.00	60	4.7	12.1
	9.00	306	23.7	35.9
	10.00	230	17.8	53.7
	11.00	234	18.1	71.8
	12.00	150	11.6	83.4
	13.00	114	8.9	92.3
	14.00	52	4.0	96.3
	15.00	29	2.3	98.6
	16.00	18	1.4	100.0

The relative majority of respondents are clustered around the "9" to "12" points scores, thus indicating that some 900 plus respondents might be harboring concurrent appreciation of authoritarian and democratic political systems. This result suggested that particular attention was needed to set appropriate cut-off points to quartile the scale to ensure each quartiled group was distinctly different from the other. Following a series of cross-tabulations to identify distinctive features of the four groups, the cut-off points for the four levels of the ID Democracy Scale were set as follows:

a. *Low* – includes original scores between "4" and "9" and identifies respondents with strong authoritarian attitudes;
b. *Low to Medium* – includes the original score of "10" and identifies respondents whose attitudes are borderline authoritarian;
c. *Medium to High* – includes scores between "11" and "12" and identifies respondents whose attitudes are borderline democratic;
d. *High* – includes the scores between "13" and "16" and identifies respondents with strong democratic attitudes.

Annex 2.14. Indonesia 2011 democratic scale

	Frequency	Percentage
System Missing	49	3.8
Low (i.e. Strong Authoritarian)	414	32.1
Low to Medium (i.e. Borderline Authoritarian)	230	17.8
Medium to High (i.e. Borderline Democrat)	384	29.7
High (i.e. Strong Democrat)	214	16.6
Total	**1290**	**100.0**

Annex 2.15. Indonesia 2011 summary results for correlations and significance of association for the ID 2011 democracy scale

	Pearson Chi Square	Theil's U
Maintain significance at the 0.05 level, with Theil's U values equal or above 15 percentage		
Age	0.000	0.036
Knowledge of Democratic Countries in Asia	0.000	0.027
Knowledge of Authoritarian Countries in Asia	0.000	0.040
Maintain significance at the 0.05 level, with Theil's U values below 15 percentage		
Urban and Rural Status	0.016	0.007
Education	0.000	0.008
Individual Perception of ID Macro-economic Outlook	0.000	0.013
Perception of Current ID Macro-economic Outlook	0.000	0.013
Perception of Retrospective ID Macro-economic Outlook	0.000	0.014
Perception of Prospective ID Macro-economic Outlook	0.000	0.014
Individual Consumption of Consumers Goods	0.000	0.014
Individual Ownership of Durable Goods	0.009	0.006
Modern Opinion Leader/Traditional Advisors	0.000	0.014
Interest in Politics	0.017	0.005
Political Party Membership	0.010	0.010
Media Exposure	0.005	0.008
Trust in the Media	0.007	0.005
Social Capital Formation	0.000	0.012
Dispute Resolution	0.000	0.010
Non-electoral Participation	0.029	0.004
Attitudes toward Elections	0.006	0.004
Fail to maintain significance at the 0.05 level		
Political Knowledge	0.234	
Gender	0.337	
Opinion Leader	0.096	
Advisor	0.103	
Advisee	0.248	
Advisor/Advisee	0.134	
Participation in Political Parties Activities	0.245	
CSOs Membership and Participation	0.329	

Annex 2.16. Summary results for logistic regression model for Indonesia 2011 democracy scale

	Low				Low to Medium				Medium to High			
	B	SE	Exp(B)	Sig	B	SE	Exp(B)	Sig	B	SE	Exp(B)	Sig
Individual perception of Indonesia macro-economic outlook												
Right Direction	.576	.192	1.910	.003	.154	.210	1.166	.465	.032	.188	.865	.968
Wrong Direction	.456	.202	1.763	.000	.245	.350	1.256	.665	.113	.202	.654	.765
Individual consumption of consumer goods												
More/Just the Same	-.804	.289	.447	.005	-.571	.324	.565	.078	-.533	.303	.587	.078
Mixed	-1.013	.334	.363	.002	-.187	.354	.829	.597	-.042	.325	.959	.897
Declining	-1.119	.307	.327	.000	-.656	.337	.519	.052	-.551	.312	.577	.077
Severely Declined	-.770	.311	.463	.013	-.624	.351	.536	.075	-.016	.311	.666	.958
Stopped Buying/Never Bought	-.654	.325	.488	.005	-.595	.332	.555	.111	-.116	.309	.567	.125
Social capital formation												
Non-group Response	.733	.199	2.081	.000	.860	.218	2.362	.000	.111	.203	1.118	.582
Group Response	.753	.227	2.195	.005	.750	.195	2.501	.000	.217	.222	1.211	.115

Regression reference category: Strong Democratic Attitudes
Chi Square = 193.99
N = 1,093
Cox and Snell R^2 = 21.8%
Nagelkerke R^2 = 28.4%

Korea democratic and authoritarian affective support

Annex 2.17. Korea 2011 democracy scale raw scores

		Frequency	Percent	Cumulative Percent
Valid	4.00	12	1.4	1.4
	5.00	12	1.4	2.8
	6.00	30	3.5	6.3
	7.00	95	11.2	17.5
	8.00	165	19.1	37.2
	9.00	145	17.0	54.2
	10.00	153	18.0	72.2
	11.00	73	8.6	80.8
	12.00	41	4.8	85.6
	13.00	53	6.0	91.6
	14.00	20	3.1	94.7
	15.00	18	2.3	97.0
	16.00	18	3.0	
Total		**850**	**100.0**	

Following a series of cross-tabulations to identify distinctive features of the four groups, the cut-off points for the four levels of the SK 2011 Democracy Scale were set as follows:

a. *Low* includes original scores between "4" and "9" and identifies respondents with strong authoritarian attitudes;
b. *Low to Medium* includes the original score of "10" and identifies respondents whose attitudes are borderline authoritarian;
c. *Medium to High* includes original scores between "11" and "12"; and identifies respondents whose attitudes are borderline democratic;
d. *High* includes scores between "13" and "16" and identifies respondents with strong democratic attitudes.

Annex 2.18. Marginal distribution for Korea 2011 scale of democratic and authoritarian attitudes

	Frequency	Percentage	Cumulative Percentage
Low (i.e. Strong Authoritarian)	462	54.0	54.0
Low to Medium (i.e. Borderline Authoritarian)	153	17.8	71.8
Medium to High (i.e. Borderline Democrat)	114	13.2	85.0
High (i.e. Strong Democrat)	121	15.0	
Total	**850**	**100.0**	

Annex 2.19. Summary results for correlations and significance of association for the Korea 2011 democracy scale

	Pearson Chi Square	Theil's U
Maintain significance at the 0.05 level with Theil's U values equal or above 15 percentage		
Knowledge of Authoritarian Countries in Asia	0.000	0.023
Retrospective Perception of SK Macro-economic Outlook	0.000	0.021
Individual Perception of SK Macro-economic Outlook	0.000	0.018
Individual Consumption of Consumers Goods	0.001	0.015
Non-electoral Participation	0.000	0.015
Maintain significance at the 0.05 level with Theil's U values below 15 percentage		
Opinion Leader/Advisors	0.000	0.014
Perception of SK Current Macro-economic Outlook	0.000	0.014
Political Knowledge	0.000	0.013
Urban/Rural Status	0.000	0.012
Knowledge of Democratic Countries in Asia	0.012	0.012
Trust in the Media	0.001	0.011
Perception of SK Prospective Macro-economic Outlook	0.006	0.009
Dispute Resolution	0.004	0.009
Education	0.013	0.007
CSOs Participation	0.014	0.007
Attitudes toward Elections	0.010	0.007
Social Capital Formation	0.022	0.005
Opinion Leaders	0.025	0.004
Advisee	0.045	0.004
Advisor/Advisee	0.031	0.004
Ownership of Durable Goods	0.045	0.007
Fail to maintain significance at the 0.05 level		
Age	0.109	
Media Exposure	0.189	
Advisor	0.068	
Interest in Politics	0.595	

Annex 2.20. Summary results for logistic regression model for Korea 2011 democracy scale

	Low				Low to Medium				Medium to High			
	B	SE	Exp(B)	Sig	B	SE	Exp(B)	Sig	B	SE	Exp(B)	Sig
Individual perception of Indonesia macro-economic outlook												
Right Direction	1.137	.273	3.515	.000	.532	.259	1.503	.040	.154	.282	1.366	.586
Wrong Direction	.852	.193	2.711	.005	.475	.235	1.835	.035	.237	.351	1.111	.357
Non-electoral participation												
No Participation	.834	.316	1.434	.008	.646	.316	1.524	.041	.257	.322	1.533	.024
Low Participation	.209	.342	1.811	.041	.756	.314	1.124	.037	.672	.324	1.159	.015
High Participation	.235	.356	1.650	.045	.615	.295	1.365	.025	.594	.310	1.405	.037

Regression reference category: **Strong Democratic Attitudes**
Chi Square = 65.726
N = 850
Cox and Snell R² = 12.9%
Nagelkerke R² = 21.8%

Thailand democratic and authoritarian affective support

Annex 2.21. Thailand 2011 democracy scale raw scores

		Frequency	Percentage	Cumulative Percentage
Valid	System Missing	51	5.6	5.6
	4.00	8	.9	6.5
	5.00	5	.5	7.0
	6.00	7	.8	7.8
	7.00	27	3.0	10.8
	8.00	55	6.1	17.0
	9.00	225	25.1	42.0
	10.00	179	19.9	61.9
	11.00	144	16.0	77.9
	12.00	88	9.8	87.7
	13.00	52	5.8	93.5
	14.00	24	2.7	96.1
	15.00	16	1.8	97.9
	16.00	18	2.1	100.0
	Total	**900**	**100.0**	

Following a series of cross-tabulations to identify distinctive features of the four groups, the cut-off points for the four levels of the TH 2011 Democracy Scale were set as follows:

a. *Low,* which includes original scores between "4" to "9" and identifies respondents with strong authoritarian attitudes;
b. *Low to Medium,* which includes the original score of "10" and identifies respondents whose attitudes are borderline authoritarian;
c. *Medium to High,* which includes original scores between "11" and "12"; and identifies respondents whose attitudes are borderline democratic;
d. *High, which* includes scores between "13" and "16" and identifies respondents with strong democratic attitudes;

Annex 2.22. Thailand 2011 democracy scale

	Frequency	Percentage	Cumulative Percentage
System Missing	51	5.6	5.6
Low (i.e. Strong Authoritarian)	327	36.4	42.0
Low to Medium (i.e. Borderline Authoritarian)	179	19.9	61.9
Medium to High (i.e. Borderline Democrat)	232	25.8	87.7
High (i.e. Strong Democrat)	111	12.3	100.0
Total	**900**	**100.0**	

Annex 2.23. Summary results for correlations and significance of associations for Thailand 2011 democracy scale

	Pearson Chi Square	Theil's U
Maintain significance at the 0.05 level with Theil's U values equal or above 15 percentage		
Exposure to Media	0.000	0.015
Dispute Resolution	0.000	0.030
Non-electoral Participation	0.040	0.022
Individual perception of TH Macro-economic Outlook	0.000	0.019
Knowledge of Authoritarian Countries in Asia	0.000	0.037
Knowledge of Democratic Countries in Asia	0.000	0.030
Attitudes toward Elections	0.000	0.020
Trust in the Media	0.000	0.015
Participation in Political Parties Activities	0.000	0.015
Maintain significance at the 0.05 level with Theil's U values below 15 percentage		
Participation in CSOs	0.011	0.008
Gender	0.046	0.012
Age	0.023	0.012
Education	0.010	0.014
Modern Opinion Leader/Traditional Advisor	0.026	0.009
Modern Opinion Leader	0.004	0.008
Social Capital Formation	0.012	0.007
Political Knowledge	0.001	0.010
Urbanity	0.000	0.014
Fail to maintain significance at the 0.05 level		
Advisor	0.433	
Advisee	0.355	
Advisor/Advisee	0.769	
Current perception of TH Macro-economic Outlook	0.246	
Prospective perception of TH Macro-economic Outlook	0.435	
Retrospective Perception of TH Macro-economic Outlook	0.345	
Individual Consumption of Consumer Goods	0.179	
Individual Ownership of Durable Goods	0.235	
Interest in Politics	0.124	

Annex 2.24. Summary results logistic regression model for Thailand 2011 democracy scale

	Low				Low to Medium				Medium to High			
	B	SE	Exp(B)	Sig	B	SE	Exp(B)	Sig	B	SE	Exp(B)	Sig
Individual perception of Indonesia macro-economic outlook												
Right Direction	1.137	.273	3.207	.000	.532	.259	2.515	.040	.154	.282	1.266	.586
Wrong Direction	.852	.193	2.815	.005	.475	.235	1.815	.035	.237	.351	3.011	.357
Urban and rural status												
Urban – Capital City	.345	.469	1.621	.035	.584	.476	1.432	.007	.875	.234	2.216	.015
Urban non-capital	.642	.335	1.722	.015	.811	.365	1.211	.015	.579	.537	1.632	.037
Rural	.540	.316	2.234	.000	.754	.205	1.745	.035	.877	1.223	.900	.027
Attitudes toward elections												
Waste of Time	.834	.316	1.434	.558	.646	.316	2.248	.087	.257	.322	1.733	.424
Patronage	.209	.342	4.876	.006	.756	.314	4.248	.017	.672	.324	1.959	.498
Democratic Participation	.235	.356	1.365	.045	.615	.295	3.775	.025	.594	.310	2.105	.457

Regression reference category: **Strong Democratic Attitudes**
Chi Square = 102.410
N = 875
Cox and Snell R^2 = 31.5%
Nagelkerke R^2 = 42.8%

2. Spatial econometric analysis of the spread of democracy[1]

In 2009, Leeson and Dean conducted an empirical investigation to understand how democracy spreads from one country to another. Their research is one of the more systematic attempts at understanding democratic diffusion. This work builds on the work of Leeson and Sobel on capitalist contagion and the search for spatial dependence in changes in democracy across geographic neighbors over time using spatial econometrics and panel data that cover over 130 countries between 1850 and 2000. They constructed a panel of democracy scores for four different time periods: 1851–2001, 1901–2001, 1951–2001 and 1991–2001. Leeson and Dean wanted to take advantage of the fact that international democracy scores are available going back to the start of the 19th century. However, they encountered a problem when data revealed that the further back their sample went, the fewer countries it contained. The data included enough countries to construct a statistically meaningful panel that extends back to 1850. Considering four different samples that cover different time periods allows to maximize the number of years and number of countries Leeson and Dean's analysis considers, and to check if the process of democratic contagion described by the theory of diffusion may have been at work through all the four periods or just during certain periods but not others.

The econometric analysis uses spatial methods, which represent the most effective ways to estimate the spread of democracy between geographic neighbors. Unlike Ordinary Least Squares, which produce biased estimates in the face of spatial correlation, spatial methods are designed specifically to identify and measure spatial dependence. If there is spatial dependence between countries' changes in democracy, spatial econometric methods can identify it and estimate the value of this dependence. Leeson and Dean's analysis uses two spatial econometric models: a spatial autoregressive model (SAR) and a spatial error model (SEM).

The SAR model specifies each country's dependent variable (which in the case of Leeson and Dean is "change in democracy") as a function of the weighted value of the changes in democracy in its neighbors. The SAR model allows potential democracy spillovers to flow multi-directionally

---

[1] The information presented in this section of Annex 2 draws and is adapted from: Peter T. Leeson and Andrea M. Dean. 2009. The Democratic Domino Theory: An Empirical Investigation. American Journal of Political Science. Vol. 53, No. 3, pp. 533–551; and John O'Loughlin, Michael D. Ward, Corey L. Lofdahl, Jordin S. Cohen, David S. Brown, David Reilly, Kristian S. Gleditsch and Michael Shin. 1998. The Diffusion of Democracy, 1946–1994. Annals of the Association of American Geographers. Vol. 88, No. 4, pp. 545–574.

rather than uni-directionally as it would happen if an auto-regressive time-series model were to be used. This is important since Deen and Leeson were interested in how changes in democracy may flow into and out of multiple countries, influencing the extent of democracy in each nation. The SAR model takes the form of $\Delta D_t = \alpha + \rho W \Delta D_t + D_{t-5}\beta + X\omega + v_t$, where ΔD_t measures countries' changes in democracy between year t and year $t - 4$. The model considers countries' changes in democracy over four-year periods to allow sufficient time for possible changes in countries' democracy to occur. W is a spatial weight matrix based on first-degree contiguity; that is taking into account bordering geographic neighbors. For example, the United States has two contiguous geographic neighbors, Canada and Mexico, so each of these countries receives a weight of 1/2 in the spatial weight matrix W as America's geographic neighbors. Finally, ρ is the model spatial autoregressive coefficient and measures the spread of democracy between geographic neighbors. If democracy spreads across countries, this coefficient is expected to be positive and significant. The SAR model also includes countries' lagged levels of democracy to control for as many factors as possible besides democratic contagion that might affect changes in democracy in its geographic neighbors. This variable accounts for the fact that geographic neighbors often share a similar colonial and/or legal origin, form of government and other factors that tend to persist over time. It also controls for features that contribute to changes in democracy, which were present the year before the period during possible democratic changes are investigated. The "lagged democracy" variable is also allows to test whether "democratic convergence" happens. That is testing whether countries with lower levels of democracy in an earlier time-period experience a faster democratic growth in the following time-period. Opposite to this, if countries with lower levels of democracy in an earlier time-period experience a slower democratic growth in the following period, these countries would be experiencing "democratic divergence."

The SEM model takes the form of: $\Delta D_t = \alpha + D_{t-5}\beta + X\omega + \varepsilon_t; \lambda W \Delta \varepsilon_t + \eta_t$, where λ is the spatial autocorrelation coefficient, which measures the spread of democracy. The SEM model specifies each country's error term, which in Leeson and Dean's model is changes in democracy, as a function of the weighted value of the changes in democracy error term of the country's geographic neighbors. Like the SAR model, the SEM model also allows potential democracy spillovers to flow multi-directionally rather than just uni-directionally.

Annex 2.25. List of countries used in the SAR and SEM analyses

	1950	1990	2000	2010
Albania	X	X	X	X
Algeria		X	X	X
Angola		X	X	X
Argentina	X	X	X	X
Australia	X	X	X	X
Austria	X	X	X	X
Bahrain		X	X	X
Belgium	X	X	X	X
Benin	X	X	X	X
Bhutan	X	X	X	X
Bolivia	X	X	X	X
Brazil	X	X	X	X
Bulgaria		X	X	X
Burkina Faso		X	X	X
Burundi		X	X	X
Cambodia		X	X	X
Cameroon		X	X	X
Canada	X	X	X	X
Central African Republic		X	X	X
Chad	X	X	X	X
Chile	X	X	X	X
China	X	X	X	X
Colombia		X	X	X
Comoros		X	X	X
Congo, Democratic Rep.		X	X	X
Congo, Republic of	X	X	X	X
Costa Rica	X	X	X	X
Cuba		X	X	X
Cyprus	X	X	X	X
Czech Republic	X	X	X	X
Denmark	X	X	X	X
Djibouti		X	X	X
Dominican Republic	X	X	X	X
Ecuador	X	X	X	X
Egypt	X	X	X	X
El Salvador		X	X	X
Equatorial Guinea		X	X	X

(Continued)

Annex 2.25. (Continued)

	1950	1990	2000	2010
Ethiopia	X	X	X	X
Fiji		X	X	X
Finland	X	X	X	X
France	X	X	X	X
Gabon		X	X	X
Gambia		X	X	X
Germany		X	X	X
Ghana		X	X	X
Greece	X	X	X	X
Guatemala	X	X	X	X
Guinea		X	X	X
Guinea Bissau		X	X	X
Guyana		X	X	X
Haiti	X	X	X	X
Honduras	X	X	X	X
Hungary		X	X	X
India	X	X	X	X
Indonesia	X	X	X	X
Iran	X	X	X	X
Iraq	X	X	X	X
Ireland	X	X	X	X
Israel	X	X	X	X
Italy	X	X	X	X
Ivory Coast		X	X	X
Jamaica		X	X	X
Japan	X	X	X	X
Jordan		X	X	X
Kenya	X	X	X	X
Korea, North		X	X	X
Korea, South		X	X	X
Laos		X	X	X
Lesotho	X	X	X	X
Liberia		X	X	X
Libya		X	X	X
Madagascar		X	X	X
Malawi		X	X	X
Malaysia		X	X	X
Mali		X	X	X

Annex 2.25. (Continued)

	1950	1990	2000	2010
Mauritania		X	X	X
Mauritius	X	X	X	X
Mexico	X	X	X	X
Mongolia		X	X	X
Morocco		X	X	X
Mozambique	X	X	X	X
Myanmar		X	X	X
Namibia	X	X	X	X
Nepal	X	X	X	X
Netherlands	X	X	X	X
New Zealand	X	X	X	X
Nicaragua	X	X	X	X
Niger		X	X	X
Nigeria		X	X	X
Norway	X	X	X	X
Oman	X	X	X	X
Pakistan	X	X	X	X
Panama	X	X	X	X
Papua New Guinea	X	X	X	X
Paraguay	X	X	X	X
Philippines	X	X	X	X
Poland	X	X	X	X
Portugal	X	X	X	X
Qatar		X	X	X
Romania	X	X	X	X
Russia	X	X	X	X
Rwanda		X	X	X
Saudi Arabia	X	X	X	X
Senegal		X	X	X
Sierra Leone		X	X	X
Singapore		X	X	X
Somalia		X	X	X
South Africa	X	X	X	X
Spain	X	X	X	X
Sri Lanka		X	X	X
Sudan		X	X	X
Swaziland	X	X	X	X
Sweden	X	X	X	X

(Continued)

Annex 2.25. (Continued)

	1950	1990	2000	2010
Switzerland	X	X	X	X
Taiwan		X	X	X
Tanzania		X	X	X
Thailand	X	X	X	X
Togo		X	X	X
Trinidad & Tobago		X	X	X
Tunisia		X	X	X
Turkey	X	X	X	X
United Arab Emirates		X	X	X
Uganda		X	X	X
UK	X	X	X	X
USA	X	X	X	X
Uruguay	X	X	X	X
Venezuela	X	X	X	X
Vietnam		X	X	X
Yemen		X	X	X
Yugoslavia	X	X	X	X
Zambia		X	X	X
Zimbabwe		X	X	X

Bibliography

Acemoglu, Daron and James A. Robinson. 2005. Economic Origins of Dictatorship and Democracy. Cambridge, UK: Cambridge University Press.

Acharya, Amitav. 2003. "Democratization and the Prospects for Participatory Regionalism in Southeast Asia". Third World Quarterly. Vol. 24, No. 2, pp. 375–390.

Achen, Christopher. 2005. "Two-Step Hierarchical Estimation: Beyond Regression Analysis". Political Analysis. Vol. 13, No. 4, pp. 447–456.

Agnew, J. A. 1993. The United States and American Hegemony. In P. J. Taylor (Ed.). The Political Geography of the Twentieth-Century: A Global Analysis, pp. 207–238. London, UK: Belhaven Press.

Alagappa, Muthiah. 2004. Civil Society and Political Change in Southeast Asia: Expanding and Contracting Democratic Space. Stanford, CA: Stanford University Press.

Aldrich, John A. 1993. "Rational Choice and Turnout". American Journal of Political Science. Vol. 37, No. 1, pp.: 246–278.

Alesina, Alberto and Howard Rosenthal. 1995. Partisan Politics, Divided Government and the Economy. Cambridge, UK: Cambridge University Press.

Almond, Gabriel A. and Sidney Verba. 1965. The Civic Culture: Political Attitudes and Democracy in Five Nations. Boston, MA: Little, Brown and Company.

Alvarez R. Michael, Jonathan Nagler and Jennifer R. Willette. 2000. "Measuring the Relative Impact of Issues and the Economy in Democratic Elections". Electoral Studies. Vol. 19, pp. 237–253.

Amitav, Acharya. 2004. "How Ideas Spread: Whose Norms Matter? Norm Localization and Institutional Change in Asian Regionalism". International Organization. Vol. 58, No. 2, pp. 239–275.

Amsden, Alice H. 1989. Asia's Next Giant: South Korea and Late Industrialization. New York, NY and Oxford, UK: Oxford University Press.

Anderson, Benedict. 1991. Imagined Communities: Reflections on the Origin and Spread of Nationalism. London, UK: Verso.

Anderson, Benedict. 1996. "Elections and Participation in Three Southeast Asian Countries". In R. H. Taylor (Ed.), The Politics of Elections in Southeast Asia. Cambridge, UK: Cambridge University Press.

Anderson, Christopher J. 1995. Blaming the Government: Citizens and the Economy in Five European Democracies. Armonk, NY: Sharpe.

Bibliography

Anderson, Christopher J. 2000. "Economic Voting and Political Context: A Comparative Perspective". Electoral Studies, Vol. 19, No. 2, pp. 151–170.

Anderson, Christopher and Christian Guillory. 1997. "Political Institutions and Satisfaction with Democracy: A Cross-National Analysis of Consensus and Majoritarian Systems". American Science Review. Vol. 91, No. 1, pp. 66–81.

Aspinall, Edward. 2013. "The Irony of Success in Indonesia". In Larry Diamond, Marc F. Plattner and Yun-han Chu, Democracy in East Asia. A New Century. Baltimore, MD: Johns Hopkins University Press.

Banfield, Edward. 1965. The Moral Basis of a Backward Society. Glencoe, NY: Free Press.

Barber, Benjamin. 1984. Strong Democracy: Participatory Politics for a New Age. Berkeley, CA: University of California Press.

Barnes, Samuel H. and Max Kaase. 1979. Political Action: Mass Participation in Five Western Democracies. Beverly Hills, CA: Sage.

Barry, Brian. 1978. Sociologist, Economists and Democracy. Chicago, IL: The Chicago University Press.

Bedeski, Robert E. 1994. The Transformation of South Korea. London, UK: Routledge.

Bendor, Jonathan and Dilip Mookherjee. 1987. "Institutional Structure and the Logic of Ongoing Collective Action". American Political Science Review. Vol. 81, No. 1, pp. 129–154.

Berelson, Bernard R., Paul F. Lazarsfeld and William N. McPhee. 1954. Voting: A Study of Opinion Formation in a Presidential Campaign. Chicago, IL: The University of Chicago Press.

Berman, Sheri. 1997. "Civil Society and the Collapse of the Weimar Republic". World Politics. Vol. 49, pp. 401–429.

Berry, William D. and Brady Baybeck. 2005. "Using Geographic Information Systems to Study Interstate Competition", American Political Science Review. Vol. 99, No. 4, pp. 505–519.

Bertrand, Jacques. 1998. "Review: Growth and Democracy in Southeast Asia". Comparative Politics. Vol. 30, No. 3, pp. 355–375.

Blondel, Jean. 2006. "Parties and Party Systems in East and Southeast Asia" in Ian Marsh (Ed.), Democratisation, Governance and Regionalism in East and Southeast Asia. London, UK: Routledge.

Boehmke, Frederick J. and Richard Witmer. 2004. "Disentangling Diffusion: The Effects of Social Learning and Economic Competition on State Policy Innovation and Expansion", Political Research Quarterly. Vol. 57, No. 1, pp. 39–51.

Brady, Henry E., Kay Lehman Schlozman, Sidney Verba and Laurel Elms. 1998. "Who Bowls? Class, Race, and Changing Participatory Equality". Annual Meeting of the American Political Science Association, September 3–6.

Bratton, M. and R. Mattes 2000. "Support for Democracy in Africa: Intrinsic or Instrumental". Afrobarometer Working Papers No. 1.

Bratton, M. and Robert Mattes. 2001. "Support for Democracy in Africa: Intrinsic or Instrumental?". British Journal of Political Science. Vol. 31, No. 3, pp. 447–474.

Bibliography 143

Bratton Michael, Robert Mattes and E. Gyimah-Boadi. 2005. Public Opinion, Democracy, and Market Reform in Africa. Cambridge, UK: Cambridge University Press.

Brinks, Daniel and Michael Coppedge. 2001. "Patterns of Diffusion in the Third Wave of Democracy". Annual Meetings of the American Political Science Association, 2001.

Brinks, Daniel and Michael Coppedge. 2006. "Diffusion is No Illusion: Neighbor Emulation in the Third Wave of Democracy". Comparative Political Studies. Vol. 39, No. 4, pp. 463–489.

Carlin, R. E. and M. M. Singer. 2011. "Support for Polyarchy in the Americas". Comparative Political Studies. Vol. 44, No. 11, pp. 1500–1526.

Carnaghan, Ellen. 2011. "The Difficulty of Measuring Support for Democracy in a Changing Society: Evidence from Russia". Democratization. Vol. 18, No. 3, pp. 682–706.

Chesterman, Simon. 2004. "Building Democracy through Benevolent Autocracy: Consultation and Accountability in UN Transitional Administrations". In Edward Newman and Roland Rich (Ed.), The UN Role in Promoting Democracy: Between Ideals and Reality. Tokyo, Japan: United Nations University Press.

Chu Yun-han, Larry Diamond and Andrew J. Nathan. 2008. How Asians View Democracy. New York, NY: Columbia University Press.

Collier, David and Steven Levitsky. 1997. "Democracy with Adjectives: Conceptual Innovation in Comparative Research". World Politics. Vol. 49, pp. 430–439.

Converse, P. E. 1964. "The Nature of Belief Systems in Mass Publics". In D. Apter (Ed.), Ideology and Discontent. Toronto, Canada: The Free Press of Glencoe.

Conway, Margaret. 1985. Political Participation in the United States. Washington, DC: Congressional Quarterly, Inc.

Coppedge, Michael. 2002. "Democracy and Dimensions. Comments on Munck and Verkuilen". Comparative Political Studies. Vol. 35, No. 1, pp. 35–39.

Cotton, James. 2007. "Timor-Leste and the Discourse of State Failure". Australian Journal of International Affairs. Vol. 61, No. 4, pp 455–470.

Croissant, Aurel. 2002. "Electoral Politics in Southeast and East Asia: A Comparative Perspective". In Aurel Croissant, Gabriele Bruns and Marei John (Eds.), Electoral Politics in Southeast and East Asia. Singapore: Friedrich Ebert Stiftung.

Croissant, Aurel and Paul Chambers. 2010. Unraveling Intra-Party Democracy in Thailand. Asian Journal of Political Science. Vol. 18, No. 2, pp. 195–223.

Crotty, William J., Donald M. Freeman and Douglas S. Gatlin (Eds.). 1971. Political Parties and Political Behavior. Boston, MA: Allyn and Bacon.

Crouch Harold and James W. Morely. 1999. "The Dynamics of Political Change". In James W. Morley (Ed.), Driven by Growth: Political Change in the Asia-Pacific Region Armonk. New York, NY: M.E. Sharpe.

Cumings, Bruce. 1997. Korea's Place in the Sun: A Modern History. New York, NY: W.W. Norton & Company.

Dahl, Robert A. 1971. Polyarchy. New Haven, CT: Yale University Press.

Dahl, Robert A. 1989. Democracy and Its Critics. New Haven, CT: Yale University Press.

Bibliography

Dahl, Robert A. 1997. "Development and Democratic Culture". In Larry Diamond, Marc F. Plattner, Yun-han Chu and Hung-mao Tien (Eds.), Consolidating the Third Wave Democracies. Baltimore, MD: Johns Hopkins University Press.

Dalton, R., Doh Chull Shin and Willy Jou. 2007. "Understanding Democracy: Data from Unlikely Places". Journal of Democracy. Vol. 18, No. 4, pp. 142–156.

Dalton, R. J. 1994. "Communists and Democrats: Democratic Attitudes in the Two Germanies". British Journal of Political Science. Vol. 24, No. 4, pp. 469–493.

Dalton, Russell. 1999. "Political Support in Advanced Industrial Democracies". In Pippa Norris (Ed.), Critical Citizens. New York, NY: Oxford University Press.

Dalton, Russel J. and Doh Chull Shin. 2006. "Political Culture and Political Change". In Russel J. Dalton and Doh Chull Shin (Eds.), Citizens, Democracy and Markets Around the Pacific Rim. Oxford, UK: Oxford University Press.

Damarys, Canache. Forthcoming. "Citizens' Conceptualization of Democracy: Structural Complexity, Substantive Content, and Political Significance". Comparative Political Studies.

Diamond, Larry. 1992. "Economic Development and Democracy Reconsidered". American Behavioral Scientist. Vol. 35, No. 4–5, pp. 450–499.

Diamond, Larry. 1994. "Towards Democratic Consolidation" Journal of Democracy. Vol. 3, pp. 36–51.

Diamond, Larry. 1998. "Introduction, Persistence, Erosion, Breakdown and Renewal". In Diamond, Larry, Juan Linz and Seymour Martin Lipset (Eds.), Democracy in Developing Countries: Asia. Boulder, CO: Lynne Rienner Publishers.

Diamond, Larry. 1998. "Is the Third Wave Over?" Journal of Democracy. Vol. 7, No. 3, pp. 20–37.

Diamond, Larry. 1999. Developing Democracy: Toward Consolidation. Baltimore, MD: Johns Hopkins University Press.

Diamond, Larry and Gi-wook Shin (Eds.). 2014. New Challenges for Maturing Democracies in Korea and Taiwan. Stanford, CA: Stanford University Press.

Diamond, Larry Jay and Marc F. Plattner. 2008. How People View Democracy. Baltimore, MD: Johns Hopkins University Press.

Di Palma, Giuseppe. 1990. To Craft Democracies: An Essay on Democratic Transitions. Berkeley, CA: University of California Press.

Doh, Chull Shin. 1994. "On the Third Wave of Democratization: A Synthesis of Recent Theory and Research". World Politics. Vol. 47, No. 1, pp. 135–70.

Doh, Chull Shin, Russell Dalton and Yun-han Chu. 2008. "Citizens, Political Parties, and Democratic Development". In Russell Dalton, Doh Chull Shin and Yun-han Chu (Eds.), Party Politics in East Asia: Citizens, Elections and Democratic Development. Boulder and London, UK: Lynne Rienner.

Duch, Raymond M. 1991. "Tolerating Economic Reform: Popular Support for Transition to a Free Market in Republics of the Former Soviet Union". Houston: TX, University of Houston.

Duch, Raymond M. 1995. "Economic Chaos and the Fragility of Democratic Transition in Former Communist Regimes". The Journal of Politics. Vol. 57, No. 1, pp. 21–158.

Bibliography

Duch, Raymond M. 1998. "The Electoral Connection and Democratic Transition". Electoral Studies. Vol. 7, No. 2, pp. 149–174.

Duch, Raymond M. 2001. "A Developmental Model of Heterogeneous Economic Voting in New Democracies". The American Political Science Review. Vol. 95, No. 4, pp. 895–910.

Duch, Raymond M. and Randy Stevenson. 2005. "Context and the Economic Vote: A Multilevel Analysis". Political Analysis. Vol. 13, No. 4, pp. 387–409.

Duch, Raymond M. and Michaell A. Taylor. 1993. "Post-Materialism and the Economic Condition" American Journal of Political Science. Vol. 37, pp. 747–778.

Duch, Raymond M., Harvey D. Palmer and Christopher J. Anderson. 2000. "Heterogeneity in Perceptions of National Economic Conditions". American Journal of Political Science. Vol. 44, No. 4, pp. 635–652.

Easton, D. 1965. A Systems Analysis of Political Life. New York, NY: John Wiley.

Eckert, Carter J., Ki-baik Lee, Young Ick Lew, Michael Robinson and Edward Wagner. 1990. Korea Old and New: A History. Seoul, Korea: Ilchokak, Publishers.

Eckstein, H. 1961. A Theory of Stable Democracy. Princeton: Princeton University Press.

Evans, G. A. and S. Whitefield. 1995. "The Politics and Economics of Democratic Commitment: Support for Democracy in Transition Societies". British Journal of Political Science. Vol. 25, No. 4, pp. 485–514.

Ferejohn, John A. and Morris P. Fiorina. 1974. "The Paradox of Not Voting: A Decision Theoretic Analysis". American Political Science Review. Vol., 68, pp. 525–535.

Finkel, Steve, Christopher Sabatini and Gwendolyn Bevis. 2000. "Civic Education, Civic Society, and Political Mistrust in a Developing Democracy: The Case of the Dominic Republic". World Development. Vol. 28, No. 11, pp. 1851–1874.

Finnemore, Martha and Kathryn Sikkink. 1998. "International Norm Dynamics and Political Change". International Organization. Vol. 52, No. 4, pp. 887–917.

Fiorina, Morris. 1978. "Economic Retrospective Voting in American National Elections: A Micro-Analysis". American Journal of Political Science. Vol. 22, No. 2, pp. 426–443.

Florini, Ann. 1996. "The Evolution of International Norms", International Studies Quarterly. Vol. 40, No. 3, pp. 363–389.

Fuchs, Dieter and Edeltraud Roller. 2006. Learned democracy? Support for democracy in Central and Eastern Europe. International Journal of Sociology. Vol. 36, pp: 70–96.

Fukuyama, Francis. 1992. The End of History and the Last Man. New York, NY: The Free Press.

Fukuyama, Francis. 1995. Confucianism and Democracy. Journal of Democracy. Vol. 6, No. 2, pp. 20–33.

Fukuyama, Francis. 1999. "Social Capital and Civil Society". Prepared for delivery at the International Monetary Fund Conference on Second Generation Reforms. Washington DC, October 1–5.

Bibliography

Fukuyama, Francis, Bjorn Dressel and Boo-Seung Chang. 2005. "Challenge and Change in East Asia: Facing the Perils of Presidentialism". Journal of Democracy. Vol. 16, No. 2, pp. 102–116.

Gamson, William A. 1968. Power and Discontent. Homewood, Illinois: The Dorsey Press.

Gellner, Ernest. 1983. Nations and Nationalism. Ithaca, NY: Cornell University Press.

Gibson, James L. 1996. "A Mile Wide But an Inch Deep (?): The Structure of Democratic Commitments in the Former USSR", American Journal of Political Science. Vol. 40, No. 2, pp. 396–420.

Gilley, B. 2006. "The Determinants of State Legitimacy: Results for 72 Countries". International Political Science Review. Vol. 27, No. 1, pp. 47–71.

Graham, Erin, Charles R. Shipan and Craig Volden. 2008. "The Diffusion of Policy Diffusion Research". Paper presented to the 2008 Annual Meetings of the American Political Science Association.

Greenfeld, Liah. 1992. Nationalism: Five Roads to Modernity. Cambridge, MA: Harvard University Press.

Haggard, Stephan. 2000. The Political Economy of the Asian Financial Crisis. Washington, DC: Institute for International Economics.

Haggard, Stephan and Mathew D. McCubbins. 2001. Presidents, Parliaments, and Policy Cambridge, UK: Cambridge University Press.

Hawkins, Brett W., Vincent L. Marando and George A. Taylor. 1971. "Efficacy, Mistrust, and Political Participation: Findings from Additional Data and Indicators". The Journal of Politics. Vol. 33, pp. 1130–1136.

Hellman, Joel. 1998. "Winners Take All: The Politics of Partial Reform in Postcommunist Transitions". World Politics. Vol. 50, No. 1, pp. 203–234.

Henderson, Gregory. 1968. Korea: The Politics of the Vortex. Cambridge, MA: Harvard University Press.

Hicken, Allen. 2006. "Stuck in the Mud: Parties and Party Systems in Democratic Southeast Asia". Taiwan Journal of Democracy. Vol. 2, No. 2, pp. 23–46.

Hicken, Allan. 2008. "Developing Democracies in Southeast Asia". In Erik Kuhonta, Dan Slater and Tuong Vu (Eds.), Southeast Asia in Political Science. Stanford, CA: Stanford University Press.

Hill, Stuart and Donald Rothchild. 1986. "The contagion of political conflict in Africa and the world". Journal of Conflict Resolution. Vol. 30, No. 4, pp. 716–735.

Hofferbert, R. I. and R.-D. Klingemann. 2001. "Democracy and Its Discontents in Post-Wall Germany". International Political Science Review. Vol. 22, No. 4, pp. 363–378.

Hofman, Bert and Kai Kaiser. 2002. "The Making of the Big Bang and Its Aftermath: A Political Economy Perspective". Paper presented at the conference Can Decentralization Help Rebuild Indonesia? Andrew Young School of Policy Studies, Georgia State University, May 1–3, 2002, Atlanta, GA.

Horowitz, Donald. 1985. Ethnic Groups in Conflict. Berkeley: University of California Press.

Huber, John D., Georgia Kernell, and Eduardo L. Leoni. 2005. "Institutional Context, Cognitive Resources and Party Attachments Across Democracies". Political Analysis. Vol. 13, no. 4, pp. 365–386.
Hughes, Caroline. 2009. Dependent Communities: Aid and Politics in Cambodia and East Timor. Ithaca, NY: Cornell University Press.
Huntington, Samuel P. 1968. Political Order in Changing Societies. Yale, CT: University Press.
Huntington, Samuel P. 1991. The Third Wave: Democratization in the Late Twentieth Century. Tulsa, OK: University of Oklahoma Press.
Huntington, Samuel P. 1996. The Clash of Civilizations and the Remaking of World Order. New York, NY: Simon & Schuster.
Huntington, Samuel P. 1996. "Democracy for the Long Haul". Journal of Democracy. Vol. 7, No. 2, pp. 3–13.
Huntington, Samuel P. 1996. "The West: Unique, Not Universal". Foreign Affairs. November/December, pp. 28–46.
Huntington, Samuel P. 1997. "After Twenty Years: The Future of the Third Wave". Journal of Democracy. Vol. 8, No. 4, pp. 3–12.
Inglehart, Ronald. 1977. Modernization and Postmodernization: Cultural, Economic, and Political Change in 43 Societies. Princeton, NJ: Princeton University Press.
Inglehart, Ronald. 1988. "The Renaissance of Political Culture". American Political Science Review. Vol. 82, No. 4, pp. 1203–1230.
Inglehart, Ronald and Christian Welzel. 2005. Modernization Cultural Change, and Democracy: The Human Development Sequence: Cambridge, UK: Cambridge University Press.
Inkeles, Alex and David H. Smith. 1974. Becoming Modern: Individual Change in Six Developing Countries. Cambridge, MA: Harvard University Press.
International Monetary Fund. World Economic Outlook Report: 1998, 1999, 2000, 2001, 2002, 2003, 2004, 2005, 2006, 2007, 2008, 2009, 2010, 2011, 2012. http//:www.imf.org/external/pubs/ft/weo/2012/weodata/index.aspx
Jackman, Robert W. and Ross A. Miller. 1996. "The Poverty of Political Culture". American Journal of Political Science. Vol. 40, No. 3, pp. 697–716.
Jackman, Robert W. and Ross A. Miller. 1996. "A Renaissance of Political Culture?" American Journal of Political Science. Vol. 40, No. 3, pp. 632–659.
Jones, David Martin. 1998. "Democratization, Civil Society, and Illiberal Middle Class Culture in Pacific Asia". Comparative Politics. Vol. 30, No. 2, pp. 147–169.
Kang, Won-Taek and Hoon Jaung. 1999. "The 1997 presidential election in South Korea". Electoral Studies. Vol. 18, pp. 599–608.
Keech, William. 1995. Economic Politics and the Costs of Democracy. Cambridge, UK: Cambridge University Press.
Key, V. O. 1966. The Responsible Electorate. New York, NY: Vintage Books.
Kim, Byung-Kook. 2000. "Electoral Politics and Economic Crisis, 1997–1998". Larry Diamond and Byung-Kook Kim (Eds.). Consolidating Democracy in South Korea. Boulder, CO: Lynne Rienner Publishers.

Bibliography

Kim, Byung-Kook. 2000. "Party Politics in South Korea's Democracy: The Crisis of Success". In Larry Diamond and Byung-Kook Kim (Eds.), Consolidating Democracy in South Korea. Boulder, CO: Lynne Rienner Publishers.

Kim, Chong Lim (Ed.). 1980. Political Participation in Korea. Santa Barbara, CA: Clio Books.

Kim, Sunhyuk. 2000. The Politics of Democratization in Korea: The Role of Civil Society. Pittsburgh, PA: University of Pittsburgh Press.

Kitschelt, Herbert. 2000. "Linkages Between Citizens and Politicians in Democratic Polities". Comparative Political Studies. Vol. 33, No. 6/7, pp. 845–879.

Klingemann, Hans-Dieter. 1999. "Mapping Political Support in the 1990s: A Global Analysis". In Pippa Norris (Ed.), Critical Citizens. New York, NY: Oxford University Press.

Kunioka, T. and G. M. Woller. 1999. "In (a) Democracy We Trust: Social and Economic Determinants of Support for Democratic Procedures in Central and Eastern Europe". Journal of Socio-Economics. Vol. 28, pp. 577–596.

Langworth, Richard M. (Ed.). 2008. Churchill by Himself: The definitive Collection of Quotations. New York, NY, Public Affairs.

Lawson, Stephanie. 1993. "Conceptual Issues in the Comparative Study of Regime Change and Democratization". Comparative Politics. Vol. 25, No. 2, pp. 183–205.

Leeson, Peter T. and Andrea M. Dean. 2009. The Democratic Domino Theory: An Empirical Investigation. American Journal of Political Science. Vol. 53, No. 3, pp: 533–551.

Lerner, Daniel. 1958. The Passing of Traditional Society. New York: Free Press of Glencoe.

Lewis-Beck, Michael S. 1988. Economics and Elections: The Major Western Democracies. Ann Arbor: University of Michigan Press.

Lewis-Beck, Michael and Glenn Mitchell. 1990. "Transnational Models of Economic Voting: Tests from a Western European Pool". Revista del Instituto de Estudios Economicos. Vol. 4. pp. 65–81.

Li, Richard P. Y. and William R. Thompson. 1975. "The Coup Contagion Hypothesis". Journal of Conflict Resolution. Vol. 14, No. 1, pp. 63–88.

Liddle, William. 2002. "Indonesia's Democratic Transition: Playing by the Rules". In Reynolds, Andrew (Ed.), The Architecture of Democracy: Constitutional Design, Conflict Management and Democracy. Oxford, UK: Oxford University Press.

Lijphart, Arend. 1997. "Unequal Participation: Democracy's Unresolved Dilemma". American Political Science Review. Vol. 91, No. 1, pp. 1–14.

Lijphart, Arend and Bernard Grofman (Eds.). Choosing an Electoral System: Issues and Alternatives. New York, NY: Praeger.

Linz, Juan J. 1990. "The Perils of Presidentialism". Journal of Democracy, Vol. 1, pp. 51–69.

Linz, Juan J. and Alfred Stepan. 1996. Problems of Democratic Transition and Consolidation: Southern Europe, South America, and Post-Communist Europe. Baltimore, MD: The Johns Hopkins University Press.

Lipset, Seymour Martin. 1963. Political Man: The Social Bases of Politics. New York, NY: Anchor Books.

Lipset, Seymour Martin. 1994. "The Social Requisites of Democracy Revisited: 1993 Presidential Address". American Sociological Review. Vol. 59, pp. 1–22.
Lu, Jie. 2012. "Democratic Conceptions in East Asian Societies: A Contextualized Analysis". Paper prepared for the conference on "How the Public Views Democracy and its Competitors in East Asia: Taiwan in Comparative Perspective". Stanford University, Stanford, May 25–26, 2012.
MacIntyre, Andrew. 2003. The Power of Institutions: Political Architecture and Governance. Ithaca, NY: Cornell University Press.
Mayer J. P. 1966. De Tocqueville, Alexis. Democracy in America. New York, NY: Harper & Row.
McDougall, W. 1997. Promised Land, Crusader State: The American Encounter with the World since 1776. Boston, MA: Houghton Mifflin.
McGee, T. G. 1967. The Southeast Asian City. A Social Geography of the Primate Cities of Southeast Asia. New York, NY: Praeger Publications.
Miller, Arthur H., Vicki Miller and William Reisinger. 1997. "Conceptions of Democracy Among Mass and Elite in Post-Soviet Societies". British Journal of Political Science. Vol. 27, pp. 157–190.
Mishler, William and Richard Rose. 1996. "Trajectories of Fear and Hope-Support for Democracy in Post-Communist Europe". Comparative Political Studies. Vol. 28, No. 4, pp. 553–581
Mishler, William and Richard Rose. 2001. "Political Support for Incomplete Democracies: Realist vs. Idealist Theories and Measures". International Political Science Review. Vol. 22, No. 4, pp. 303–320.
Muller, Edward N. and Karl-Dieter Opp. 1986, June. "Rational Choice and Rebellious Collective Action". American Political Science Review. Vol. 80, No. 2, pp. 471–487.
Mutz, Diana. 1998. Impersonal Influence: How Perceptions of Mass Collectives Affect Political Attitudes. New York, NY: Cambridge University Press.
Pippa, Norris. (Ed.). 1999. Critical Citizens: Global Support for Democratic Governance. New York, NY: Oxford University Press.
O'Donnell, Guillermo A. 1973. Modernization and Bureaucratic-Authoritarianism. Berkeley, CA: University of California Press.
O'Donnell, Guillermo. 1988. "Horizontal Accountability in New Democracies". Journal of Democracy. Vol. 9, No. 3, pp. 119.
O' Donnell, Guillermo. 1996. "Illusions and Conceptual Flaws". Journal of Democracy. Vol. 7, No. 4, pp. 160–168.
O'Donnel, Guillermo and Philippe Schmitter. 1990. "Transition from Authoritarian Rule: Tentative Conclusions about Uncertain Democracies". In G. O'Donnell, Schmitter Philippe, and Lawrence Whitehead. (Eds.). 1990. Transition from Authoritarian Rule: Prospects for Democracy. Baltimore, MD: Johns Hopkins University Press.
O'Donnell, Guillermo, Philippe C. Schmitter and Laurence Whitehead (Eds.). 1986. Transitions from Authoritarian Rule: Latin America. Baltimore, MD: The Johns Hopkins University Press.

Bibliography

O'Loughlin, John, Michael D. Ward, Corey L. Lofdahl, Jordin S. Cohen, David S. Brown, David Reilly, Kristian S. Gleditsch and Michael Shin. 1998. The Diffusion of Democracy, 1946–1994. Annals of the Association of American Geographers. Vol. 88, No. 4, pp. 545–574.

Olson, Mancur. 1971. The Logic of Collective Action. Cambridge, MA: Harvard University Press.

Paige, Jeffrey. 1971. "Political Orientation and Riot Participation". American Sociological Review. Vol. 36, No. 5, pp. 810–820.

Paldam, Martin. 1991. "How Robust Is the Vote Function? A Study of Seventeen Nations over Four Decades". In Helmut Norpoth, Michael Lewis-Beck, and Jean-Dominique Lafay. (Eds.). 1991. Economics and Politics: The Calculus of Support. University of Michigan Press.

Pateman, Carole. 1970. Participation and Democratic Theory. Cambridge, UK: Cambridge University Press.

Pei, Minxin. 2003. "Rotten from Within: Decentralized Predation and the Incapacitated State". In T. V. Paul, John Ikenberry and John A. Hall (Eds.). The Nation-State in Question. Princeton, NJ: Princeton University Press.

Pompe, Sebastian. 2005. A Study of Institutional Collapse. Southeast Asia Program Publications. Ithaca, NY: Cornell University Press.

Pongsudhirak, Thitinan. 2008. "Thailand Since the Coup". Journal of Democracy. Vol. 19, No. 4, pp. 140–153.

Pongsudhirak, Thitinan. 2012. "Thailand's Uneasy Passage". Journal of Democracy. Vol. 23, No. 2, pp. 47–61.

Powell, G. Bingham, Jr. and Guy D. Whitten. 1993. "A Cross-National Analysis of Economic Voting: Taking Account of the Political Context". American Journal of Political Science. Vol. 37, No. 2, pp. 391–414.

Przeworski, Adam. 1999. "Minimalist Conceptions of Democracy: A Defense". In Ian Shapiro and Casiano Hacker-Cordon (Eds.), Democracy's Value. Cambridge, UK: Cambridge University Press.

Przeworski, Adam, Michael Alvarez, Jose Antonio Cheibub and Fernando Limongi. 1996. "What Makes Democracies Endure?" Journal of Democracy. Vol. 7, No. 1, pp. 39–55.

Przeworski Adam and Fernando Limongi. 1997. "Modernization: Theories and Facts". World Politics. Vol. 49, pp. 155–183.

Putnam, Robert D. 1995. "Bowling Alone: America's Declining Social Capital". Journal of Democracy. Vol. 6, No. 1, pp. 65–78.

Putnam, Robert D. 2000. Bowling Alone: The Collapse and Revival of American Community. New York, NY: Simon & Schuster.

Putnam, Robert D., Robert Leonardi and Raffaella Y. Nanetti. 1993. Making Democracy Work: Civic Traditions in Modern Italy. Princeton, NJ: Princeton University Press.

Pye, Lucian W. 1985. Asian Power and Politics: The Cultural Dimensions of Authority. Cambridge, MA: Harvard University Press.

Pye, Lucian W. 1990. "Political Science and the Crisis of Authoritarianism". American Political Science Review. Vol. 84, No. 1, pp: 3–19.

Pye, Lucian W. 1999. "Civility, Social Capital, and Civil Society: Three Powerful Concepts for Explaining Asia". Journal of Interdisciplinary History. Vol. 29, No. 4, pp. 763–782.

Rahn, Wendy M., John Brehm and Neil Carlson. 1999. "National Elections as Institutions for Generating Social Capital". In Theda Skocpol and Morris P. Fiorina (Eds.). Civic Engagement in American Democracy. Washington, DC: Brookings Institutions Press.

Reilly, Benjamin. 2006. Democracy and Diversity: Political Engineering in the Asia-Pacific. Oxford, UK: Oxford University Press.

Rodan, Gary. 1996. "Elections without Representation: The Singapore Experience under the PAP". In Robert H. Taylor (Ed.), The Politics of Elections in Southeast Asia. Cambridge, UK: Woodrow Wilson Center and Cambridge University Press

Rose, Richard, William Mishler and Christian Haerpfer. 1998. Democracy and Its Alternatives. Baltimore, MD: Johns Hopkins University Press.

Rueschemeyer, Dietrich. 1998. "The Self-Organization of Society and Democratic Rule: Specifying the Relationship". In Dietrich Rueschemeyer, Marilyn Rueschemeyer and Bjorn Wittrock (Eds.), Participation and Democracy East and West: Comparisons and Interpretations. Armonk, NY: M.E. Sharpe.

Rueschemeyer, Dietrich, Evelyne Huber Stephens and John D. Stephens. 1992. Capitalist Development and Democracy. Chicago, IL: University of Chicago Press.

Sartori, Giovanni. 1968. "Political Development and Political Engineering". Public Policy. Vol. 17, pp: 261–298.

Schedler, Andreas and Rodolfo Sarsfield. 2004. "Democrats with Adjectives: Linking Direct and Indirect Measures of Democratic Support". Afrobarometer Working Paper No. 45.

Schmitter, Philippe C. and Terry Lynn Karl. 1991. "What Democracy Is . . . And Is Not". Journal of Democracy. Vol. 2, No. 3, pp. 75–88.

Seligson, Amber. 1999. "Civic Association and Democratic Participation in Central America: A Test of the Putnam Thesis". Comparative Political Studies. Vol. 32, No. 3, pp. 342–362.

Shils, Edward. 1991. "The Virtue of Civil Society". Government and Opposition. Vol. 26, No. 1, pp 3–20.

Shin, Doh Chull. 1999. Mass Politics and Culture in Democratizing Korea. Cambridge: UK Cambridge University Press.

Shin, Doh Chull. 2007. "Democratization: Perspectives from Global Citizenry". In Russel Dalton and Hans-Dieter Klingemann (Eds.) The Oxford Handbook of Political Behavior. New York, NY: Oxford University Press.

Simon, Janos. 1998. "Popular Conceptions of Democracy in Postcommunist Europe". In Samuel H. Barnes and Janos Simon (Eds.), The Postcommunist Citizen. Budapest: Erasmus Foundation.

Simmons, Beth A. and Zachary Elkins. 2004. "The Globalization of Liberalization: Policy Diffusion in the International Political Economy". American Political Science Review. Vol. 98, No. 1, pp. 171–189.

Simmons, Beth A., Frank Dobbin and Geoffrey Garrett. 2006. "Introduction: The International Diffusion of Liberalism". International Organization. Vol. 60, No. 4, pp. 781–810.

Siverson, Randolph M. and Harvey Starr. 1990. "Opportunity, Willingness, and the Diffusion of War". American Political Science Review. Vol. 84, No. 1, pp. 47–67.

Slater, Dan. 2008. "Democracy and Dictatorship" in Erik Kuhonta, Dan Slater and Tuong Vu (Eds.), Southeast Asia in Political Science. Stanford, CA: Stanford University Press.

Snyder, Richard and James Mahoney. 1999. "The Missing Variable: Institutions and the Study of Regime Change". Comparative Politics. Vol. 32, No. 1, pp. 103–122.

Soule, Sarah A. 1999. "The Diffusion on an Unsuccessful Innovation". The Annals of the American Academy of Political and Social Science, Vol. 566. No. 1, pp. 120–131.

Starr, Harvey. 1991. "Democratic Dominoes: Diffusion Approaches to the Spread of Democracy in the International System". Journal of Conflict Resolution. Vol. 35, No. 2, pp. 356–381.

Steinberg, David I. 2000. "Continuing Democratic Reform: The Unfinished Symphony". In Larry Diamond and Byung-Kook Kim (Eds.), Consolidating Democracy in South Korea. Boulder, CO: Lynne Rienner Publishers.

Stepan, Alfred and Cindy Skach. 1993. "Constitutional Frameworks and Democratic Consolidation: Parliamentarianism versus Presidentialism". World Politics. Vol. 46, No. , pp. 1–22.

Stockton, Hans. 2001. "Political Parties, Party Systems, and Democracy in East Asia: Lessons from Latin America". Comparative Politics. Vol. 34, No. 1, pp. 94–119.

Streiner, D. L. and Norman, G. R. 1989. Measurement Scales: A Practical Guide to Their Development and Use. New York, NY: Oxford University Press.

Sundhaussen, Ulf. 1989. "Indonesia: Past and Present Encounters with Democracy". In Larry Diamond, Juan Linz, and Seymour Martin Lipset (Eds.), Democracy in Developing Countries: Asia. Boulder, CO: Lynne Rienner Publishers.

Tarrow, Sidney. 1998. Power in Movement: Social Movements and Contentious Politics. Cambridge, UK: Cambridge University Press.

Taylor, H. Robert. 1996. The Politics of Elections in Southeast Asia. Cambridge, UK: Woodrow Wilson Center and Cambridge University Press.

Thompson, Mark. 2004. Democratic Revolutions. Asia and Eastern Europe. London, UK: Routledge.

Toye, John. 1991. "Is There A New Political Economy of Development?" In C. Colcough and J. Manor (Eds.),States or Markets? Neo-liberalism and the Developmental Policy Debate. Oxford, UK: Clarendon Press.

Verba, Sidney. 1996. "The Citizen as Respondent: Sample Surveys and American Democracy". American Political Science Review. Vol. 90, No. 1, pp. 1–7.

Verba, Sidney and Norman H. Nie. 1972. Participation in America: Social Equality and Political Democracy. New York, NY: Harper & Row.

Verba, Sidney, Norman H. Nie, and Jae-on Kim. 1978. Participation and Political Equality: A Seven-Nation Comparison. Cambridge, UK: Cambridge University Press.

Bibliography

Verba, Sidney, Kay Lehman Schlozman and Henry E. Brady. 1995. Voice and Equality: Civic Voluntarism in American Politics. Cambridge, MA: Harvard University Press.

Verba, Sidney, Kay Lehman Schlozman, Henry E. Brady and Norman H. Nie. 1993. "Citizen Activity: Who Participates? What Do They Say?" American Political Science Review. Vol. 87, No. 2, pp. 303–318.

Whitehead, Lawrence. 1996. International Aspects of Democratization. In G. O'Donnell, P. Schmitter and L. Whitehead (Eds.), Transitions to Democracy. Baltimore, MD: Johns Hopkins University Press.

Williamson, John (Ed.). 1994. The Political Economy of Policy Reform. Washington, DC: Institute for International Economics.

World Bank. 1993. The East Asian Miracle: Economic Growth and Public Policy. World Bank Policy Research Reports. Washington, DC.

Index

Asia 1, 3, 7, 11–13, 28, 30, 34, 36, 37, 41–42, 47–48, 53, 56–57, 59, 62, 67, 69, 72, 82, 85, 98–99, 101, 109–110
authoritarianism i, viii, x, 1, 2, 5, 6–8, 10–11, 17, 22, 23–24, 28, 42–43, 56–57, 59, 61–63, 67–79, 82–90, 92–94, 96, 99–102, 109–110, 121, 125

Bangkok 2, 5, 30, 31, 33, 35, 59, 63, 75, 79–81, 93–94, 96, 99, 103–104, 107–108

democracy i, vii–x, 1–8, 9–13, 14–16, 20–23, 25, 28–29, 30, 33, 34–37, 39–41, 43–48, 50–57, 59, 61, 63, 64, 65–73, 74, 75, 79, 81–85, 86–89, 91–95, 97–102, 109–110

elections 1, 4, 5, 11, 15, 17, 18, 21–23, 25, 26–28, 30–31, 37, 40–41, 44–45, 47–48, 50–51, 55, 61, 71, 73–77, 84, 88–89, 90–94, 96, 98, 102–107, 110
elites 4–5, 10, 12, 19, 33, 44, 48, 59, 63, 67, 75, 91, 95–96, 99, 102

Jakarta 2, 4, 18, 21, 63, 75, 79, 80–81, 99, 103–104

Indonesia i, viii, ix, x, 1–8, 10–12, 14, 16–24, 34–40, 43–47, 50–52, 56–57, 59, 61–63, 67, 71–80, 82, 84, 86–89, 97–101, 103–110

institutions 4, 11–12, 14–18, 20, 22–25, 27, 33, 41, 42, 44–45, 55–56, 64, 69–70, 75, 83, 86, 89, 91, 93, 95–96, 100

Korea i–x, 1–8, 10–14, 22–30, 32–44, 46, 47–48, 50–52, 55–59, 61–63, 67, 71, 72–76, 78–80, 82, 84, 89, 90–93, 97–106

military 1, 3–5, 10, 12, 22–23, 25, 29–31, 42, 45, 48, 55, 57, 59, 71, 73–75, 82–83, 86, 89, 92–93, 95–96, 98, 110
monarchy 4, 30–32, 45, 75, 93, 95, 96

participation 1, 2, 4–5, 12–13, 21–22, 26–27, 33–37, 44, 47–48, 50–51, 59, 63–64, 84, 86, 89–94, 101, 110
  electoral participation 5, 13, 21, 26–27, 33, 37, 47–48, 50–51, 59, 63, 84, 89–91, 102, 110
  non-electoral participation 5, 13, 21, 26, 27, 31, 37, 47–48, 50, 59, 63, 77, 84, 89, 90–91, 101–102, 110
  participation in civil society organizations 5, 21–22, 30, 33–36, 44, 48, 50, 63, 77, 92, 202, 110
political/democratic cultures 6–7, 11–12, 19, 22–23, 30, 35, 37, 41, 50, 52, 59, 68, 99
political parties 4–5, 14, 16–18, 22–23, 25–26, 28, 31–33, 37, 77, 88
political systems 2, 4, 6–7, 12–13, 23, 38–39, 45–47, 57, 59, 61–64, 67, 72–29, 82–83, 94, 97, 99–100, 110

156 *Index*

social capital 35, 37, 46–47, 50, 61, 64, 84, 87, 110
Seoul 2, 57, 63, 79–81, 90–91, 99, 103–106
Thailand 2–8, 10–14, 24, 30–37, 40–43, 45, 46, 48, 50–51, 56–59, 61–61, 67, 71–72, 74–79, 82, 84, 93–108
trust 25, 46, 70, 91, 93, 110